STEPPING STONES

Daily Reflections by an
Unconventional Monk

STEPPING STONES

Daily Reflections by an
Unconventional Monk

TOLBERT MCCARROLL

Cover and Illustrations by Katelyn Wellnitz

In Memory of
Sister Marti
(1939–2016)

who was the inspiration for what appears here

There are as many paths to God as there are souls on earth.

Rumi (1207–1273)

CONTENTS

INTRODUCTION

The poet Matsuo Basho (1644–1694) had climbed high in the mountains. Great vistas surrounded him but he had been looking at his feet when he wrote;

On the mountain path,
what is this special thing?
A simple violet.

I am also a violet-seeker. And it is my hope that this book will be of use to you and others who use nature, ordinary daily life, and the ground under our feet, as signposts in finding the sacred core of existence.

Around my 80th year on this planet I realized that my faith was deeply rooted in searching for the sacred and transcendent in the environment that surrounds me. It is a simple and gentle pilgrimage in which I encounter and am enriched by other violet-seekers with different spiritual heritages and life experiences

Who am I? Like Basho, I am a lay-monk seeking a contemplative space in the busy, high-tech reality of ordinary daily life. I was raised in the tradition of Catholic spirituality, and I value it still. Am I in sync with the Vatican?

No. Somewhere in the late 20th century the centralized bureaucracy of the Roman Catholic Church imploded under a cloud of conservative ideology and institutionalism. I am part of a small, autonomous, interfaith, contemplative community called "Starcross" existing in the remote north-western corner of Sonoma County, California. We raise olives and are a crossroad for people on many spiritual paths — and none.

Like everyone else, preoccupations with very important and worthwhile matters have often made it hard for me to find the violets — as a parent, as an attorney in the struggle for civil rights, as one among many humanitarians responding to the AIDS pandemic, as an occasional religious reformer, and so on. Even when I began to walk the contemplative path of being a monk, I often felt/feel lost. It was in the incredible hellhole of children living and dying with AIDS in Romania that it became clear to me I needed a spiritual compass to help me keep from trampling those violets of Basho's. When I was a young attorney, I represented maritime unions. Much about these men and women who survive in often turbulent waters surprised me. I learned that they checked their position and their course many times a day.

There are many fogs in our lives. Holding a dying child in a heartless environment was the precise moment when I realized that I must frequently check my course to the violets. Perhaps that was the same moment this book was born.

Nature is my most reliable compass point. I attempt to follow many others, like Henry David Thoreau (1817–1862) who suggested:

Live in each season as it passes;
breathe the air, drink the drink,
taste the fruit,
and resign yourself
to the influences of each.

But there is something else. Perhaps it comes because of my age, or my religious heritage. I deeply mistrust doctrines and dogma, even from those in love with the environment. In the crazy but exciting days of the '70s in San Francisco, there were those sometimes called "the rainbow and butterfly people." Just like the religious fundamentalists, they lived in an unchanging world. However, butterflies do die and rainbows do fade away. It is from the ordinary daily experiences of those living in a changing humanity that I have learned whatever I may know about reading the compass. This is not a "New-Age" or new-anything concept. The progressive Jesuit theologian Karl Rahner (1904–1984) argued in his book *Christian in the Marketplace,* written in 1959, that the only path on which we can approach God is found in the center of ordinary, daily life.

So that is the path, the compass, the violets — the sacred and essential core of life — for me and perhaps for you.

I have been writing for the past 40 years and several people, notably my friend and agent Edite Kroll, thought that in all those words might be some little daily nudges of encouragement for those seeking to live a life in harmony with the seasons of nature and of the heart. The book you hold in your hand has grown out of those writings. This was not a simple task for someone my age, but along came Jennifer Lickteig and Katelyn Wellnitz, young and talented writers who took breathers from their own careers to sign on as the editorial associates for this book. And, with the help of my long-time companions Sister Marti Aggeler and Sister Julie DeRossi, *STEPPING STONES* was born.

Violet-seekers perhaps all begin with Basho, and we hopefully all end any year with something like this from Rainer Maria Rilke (1875–1926).

> *And you suddenly know: It was here!*
> *You pull yourself together*
> *and there stands an irrevocable year of*
> *anguish and vision and prayer.*

May it be so for you — and for me.

Tolbert McCarroll
Starcross Monastic Community
Annapolis, California

January

January 1
The Barn in Winter

The first day of the year is a great time to be in the barn. The pumpkins beside me in the loft cast a warm orange glow everywhere. Leaning over the rail I can see little evidence of the frantic activities of the recent Christmas season. The barn is very calm now. I have a warm and satisfied feeling. At times, barns are to farmers what chapels are to monks.

What calls to me most these winter days is a misty trail leading to a place where I can see life that has gone before me and, in the other direction, what is to come after me. I want to feel part of that stream. When I die, the stream will go on. That is my immortality, for I am part of an ongoing story. If our society had "elders" I would love to be one of them and share the story of our people with those who will write the next chapter.

But for today, I am simply content to stand quietly in my little barn-world.

JANUARY 2
A HOLY BONFIRE

Holiday traditions have built up over the many years in my home. Early in January, the Christmas greens are hauled to a clearing and burned.

Many thoughts come to me about the recent season as I watch the flames and the smoke rising in the air. I remember the coming together and the mirth — and arguments — as we found and cut the tree, now burning. In the crackle and the haze are moments and faces from this year and other years, when we were younger. Some, no longer with us, seem to stand happily beside us –parents who taught us to celebrate, children and friends who made life special.

Many hands throw dry wreaths and boughs on the fire. There is a pleasant warmth as the flames move through the branches. It is a thanksgiving offering for something beautiful which came, transformed, and now goes away. There is one final marvel as black limbs, white ash, and red flames create a landscape which we can discover but never inhabit. And then it is gone.

January 3
Stillness in a Changing World

L ife changes after the holidays. Refreshed, schools-busi-nesses-governments gear up. It is not just a city thing. Standing on the chapel deck, I can hear tractors in the vine-yards and chainsaws in the woods. But here at home it seems as if each day brings us into a deeper silence and peace. We are a still sanctuary in the world's race to make up for lost time. Here, for a bit, time really does seem to stand still.

Oh, there is a lot going on; flocks of birds come and go, ravens caw and hawks glide in great circles, the olive trees sway in the wind, their giant redwood neighbors dance in an awesome ballet. The sky is incredibly colorful at dawn and dusk and, unless it is raining, a bright blue during the day.

Stepping outside we are, at this time of year, a silent part-ner in our relationship to the ongoing process of creation. On my way to Vespers, the bare limbs of the fruit trees stand like monastic companions. The smoke of the wood fire in the house is our incense. The sound of the first owl pitches our chant. There is much to remember about ourselves, our friends, our world. Much to ponder about the future. But in these rare days it is also good to recall there is always something more than what we can make happen.

And, in that, often lies our hope.

January 4
When the Plant says
Nothing

The Cistercian monk Thomas Merton (1915–1968) writes in a poem, *"Love winter when the plant says nothing."* The trees around us this month cannot be valued now for their fruit, or their spring buds or their autumn foliage. There is only the unadorned, fundamental structure. We see clearly the strengths and the weaknesses.

What do we take away from this experience? Maybe only the indefinable wisdom which comes from exposure to the elemental forces of life itself. It is an insight which seems to somehow come in handy when we turn to face the big issues in our society and in our personal lives.

Merton also writes, *"O peace, bless this mad place."* The stillness, the peace, of a tree in winter can indeed bless this mad place in which we all dwell.

January 5
Twelfth Night

In medieval Europe, there was generally a truce from war which lasted through December until January 6, the feast of the Epiphany. In our own times, there is often a holiday/holyday peace from the many problems we face in coping with life, which begins to fade as we get deeper into January. I find myself stepping from the rich and glittering landscape of Christmas and back into my own homeland. The leaves are gone. The tree limbs are bare. But there is a warmth remaining which it is right to celebrate. Jesus, Mary, and Joseph have gradually morphed into the people in my own family and circle of friends. This is a hard season. Death and suffering are around us. But so is love.

In my home, we gather on this night and share the memories of this time together. We also share some of the sweet things that have been put away to be brought out again on this night!

Then we step out and silently observe the beauty of the night sky. Around us are many shadows of beings who have been, are, and will be.

January 6
The Day of the Kings

In many Christian calendars, today is the feast of the Epiphany commemorating the visit of the three magi to the home of the young Jesus. *El Dia de los Reyes,* The Day of the Kings, as our Latino neighbors call it. And, they bake wonderful round cakes — *Rosca de Reyes.* There is something valuable hidden in the cake, and that is the point.

Epiphany is a Greek word for "manifestation." — something extraordinary hidden in the ordinary lives we each live. There are many examples of how something sacred has been manifested, has broken through, into our history and times.

I learn more of what I call God has broken through into our many cultures and personal stories by discovering how we each actually go about the art of living. Each year I become more mindful of the many manifestations, epiphanies, occurring around me. It always starts with a single ordinary person, like you or me.

Shall we cut the *Rosca?*

9

January 7
The Storms of Growth

An elderly Native American once told me that the parents of all life are the sky and the earth. They come together to form a womb. Here all people, animals, and plants receive what they need to travel their paths. But, as in any birth, there is pain. Storms accompany all bornings. It is in the wild turbulence that we learn the skills for our growth.

As we travel along our paths, there must be many seasons. Without the cold and barren winter, there can be no spring beauty. Winter is the season of the womb. Its pain is our friend, our beacon. It points out the direction for our journey. Sometimes there are only two roads in life: growing and dying. The bud must go through the discomfort of unfolding, or it will shrivel.

Distress may warn us when we have broken nature's rhythm. The pain in the heart reminds us of the winter of the womb, and, again, we can prepare for a new step in life.

January 8
A Walk in Winter

E ven if our winter walk begins very early in the morning, we are coming into the middle of something. In the city, some people have been at work all night. On the dairy farm, cows have been milked before dawn. In the fields, owls are returning to their dark homes, and rabbits are completing their nocturnal adventures. In some regions, snow has been falling throughout the night.

Whatever our destination – park, forest, ocean cliff— there will be the sounds and sights of our fellow creatures. All this is sacred. Dogs bark. Cars move down the road. Emergency lights flash. Households wake. Stories are unfolding everywhere we look. The addict blocking the sidewalk or the distracted attendant at the toll booth are not just obstacles to our progress. They are companions on our journey.

What a remarkable world we enter. There is that line from the first account of the creation story in the Book of Genesis (1:31), after the sixth day: *"God saw all that had been made, and indeed it was very good."* Whatever a person's view of the Bible or of biology, the world we experience on a winter walk is "very good" – and we are part of that world.

In our quest for wholeness, wherever we walk is holy land.

January 9
The Field Beyond

Rumi (1207–1273), the Sufi poet and mystic, said something very profound, yet puzzling to the Western seeker brought up on creeds and dogma,

Out beyond ideas of right doing and wrong doing there is a field. I'll meet you there.

Once, many years ago, I was conducting a series of workshops on spiritual growth in the home. At one point, I asked the parents there what their objectives were in guiding their children. One of the most religiously traditional parents there, from a strong Roman Catholic heritage, said something that has remained with me: *"I don't want my children to grow up trying to put God in a box."* He was a wise father. Beyond the dogmas, creeds and denominations, there is a field. And all our children must find new paths through it.

January 10
On the Worst of Nights

Risk is a part of the winter season. Animals starve and freeze to death. So did our ancestors. Many ancient symbols arise from the fact that there is a physical and emotional danger inherent to the season.

Even in mild California, where I live, the wind can blow hard and cold this month. Some of my neighbors raise sheep and it often seems as if the ewes give birth to lambs on the worst nights. Some old-timers say the ewes want to bring their young forth on a night that is so bad that coyotes and other predators will not venture out. It is a nice speculation, that there is a relationship between adversity, vulnerability, and growth.

January 11
The Lover and the Monk

During my lifetime, the struggle of our age has been for freedom, and our hunger has been for peace.

We have learned there is a danger that absolute freedom, life without commitments, can lead to social isolation. We must find a balance.

In each of us there is a lover growing through active encounters with others and a monk longing for contemplative solitude. There must be balance between the monk and the lover.

The pains and the joys of life consist of experiences both in that inner space where no one else will ever enter and in the reality of our solidarity with the human community.

January 12
An Ancient Response

In our lives, there are times of primal sacred expression that override ordinary concepts of prayer. One such experience occurred at my mother's death. She died at home on a winter night. The next day friends went with me to the nearby ocean. We sat down for an hour and thought of her life. There were many little prayers and silent meditations.

On the drive home, I felt something building up inside me. My last parent was gone. There was nothing between me and history, the future, the cosmos. I felt a need to make contact with the power of life itself. I went up on a hill behind the house to a place where my mother loved to sit. It was as if her quieted spirit was laying there. I stood over that spirit facing the valley and the far hills. Then a roar began in me and erupted out of my mouth. I could not believe this was happening. A tiny part of my brain was saying, "This is bizarre!" Yet the roars kept coming out and echoed against the hills.

I was mourning in some ancient way, and it was the right thing to do. I had no doubt that my mother was in a sacred space, and for those few moments, so was I. Then there was a deep and healing silence.

January 13
Patience in the Morning

This morning there is a light fog over our farm. Walking up the hill to our little chapel, I gradually come out above the mist. Nothing is moving. There is a palpable stillness in the air. Looking back down the hill, I can see the fog drifting between the rows of our olive trees. Beneath me is probably a vast community of moles, gophers, mice, and snakes, sleeping and surviving the cold.

Not far away, icy mountain waters run through snow-covered forests. Here, the hills are frosty at dawn but green by midday. Before me, a male snowbird and a female bluebird share a branch for a few minutes and try to make sense of the world around them. Beyond them, in the clear winter sky, I see two jet trails. Perhaps some people are traveling to also make sense of their worlds. I wonder if someone is looking down, imagining there is an elderly monk contemplating two birds on a bare limb.

Ralph Waldo Emerson (1803–1882) counseled all of us to *"Adopt the pace of nature."* Some mornings it is very natural to do that.

January 14
Waxing While Waning

As I stand in the olive grove, I feel myself between the old and the new. I think back to the recent harvest and forward to the challenging months of irrigation and cultivation. My life is like this field. I am a person living with old age, prostate cancer, lack of energy and mobility, anxiety, and so it goes. We each have a list, don't we? While we are very aware of all the waning parts of life, we can nonetheless understand we are living people surrounded with fresh innocence.

On our farm we have four bird houses especially designed, supposedly, to please bluebird families. An annual January task for us is to clean out the little houses, being careful to shoo away the earwig families who have wintered there. Soon, the birds lay their eggs and watch over them.

There are fresh promises of life all around us. We are all part of that — and what has gone before, and what is yet to come as well.

January 15
Free at Last

O n the third Monday in January, most of us in the United States commemorate the life of Martin Luther King, Jr. (1929–1968). He warned of a triple scourge to freedom: poverty, racism, war. The last words of his speech during the 1963 March on Washington left us with a profound challenge to work for the time when:

> ... we will be able to speed up that day when all God's children ... will be able to join hands and sing in the words of the old Negro spiritual, "Free at last! Free at last! Thank God Almighty, we are free at last."

Since that dramatic moment, have we become more mindful of our commonness? In the years to come will we work more diligently and selflessly for the common good? Will we step away from personal privilege and confront those threats of poverty, racism, and war? I don't know.

Across the years I can hear again the clarion cry: "*So let freedom ring from the prodigious hilltops of New Hampshire ... [to] the curvaceous slopes of California!*"

And sitting on one of those slopes, I wonder, what can I do to help the process along? I have hope that if enough of us ask that question we will be able to speed up the day of which Martin Luther King, Jr. dreamed.

January 16
We do What we Can

The nights have been cold. The path to the chapel is very icy. My steps recently have not always been secure. So, I use a stick to help me walk. The garden fountain is frozen. A blue jay sits on a nearby branch, staring at the inaccessible water.

I stand here on this cold morning looking back with dissatisfaction on so many events in the years I have walked this earth. I wear a warm cap knitted by my friend the poet Lisa Jarnot (1967-) in her 100 Caps for Peace project. Mine is #65 and is worn in memory of Khalid, a 14 year-old Afghan boy gunned down by an American helicopter as he was gathering wood in the bitter cold of February 2011. Khalid was the sole support of his family of 13 sisters and 2 mothers.

How feeble it is to wear a cap, keep a picture, think about atrocious days gone by. But that is what we do as we grow older. If you haven't discovered that, you will. So we keep on remembering because, as Elie Wiesel (1928-) wrote about the Holocaust, *"To forget the dead would be akin to killing them a second time."*

Well, both the blue jay and I are still here shivering. And he is thirsty. So I take my stick and break the ice in the fountain. I hit it much more than is necessary. But you need to do that sometimes.

I walk to the chapel. The blue jay drinks. Life goes on.

January 17
A Pleasant Oasis

When the poet Emily Dickinson (1830–1886) was a schoolgirl she listened often to Edward Hitchcock (1793–1864), a president of Amherst College who found the sacred within nature. He felt it is in winter that we experience things which we may see only once in our lives. Such an event happened to the people of Amherst on January 17, 1849.

There was very cold snow, followed by a warmer night and light rain. Then it was cold again and ice formed. Hitchcock wrote, "The leafless branches and twigs of every tree, of every shrub, and even of every spire of grass were encased in this thick and beautiful crystalline coat..." And, the phenomenon repeated itself for 10 days until the colors of the prism could be seen everywhere – even by moonlight.

Somewhere in every winter, for each of us, there is something unique in nature and in life which we will rarely experience. Each of these discoveries has become, as Hitchcock put it, an event that will "be looked back upon as a pleasant oasis along the journey of life." Let us be open to that awareness.

January 18
Caring for Each Other

People of my parents' generation, coming out of the Great Depression and living between two World Wars, were want to say about catastrophic events, "These things happen."

At home this time of year, we can have day-after-day of torrential rainstorms with winds up to 75 miles an hour. There is nothing I can do about it, and there is certainly a sense of futility and depression. But I can go to the greenhouse and plant seeds. The wild tempests cannot be restrained, but I can hold the future in my hand, a tiny tomato seed, and I know that those hellish storms will not prevail against the promise of a long and delicious summer.

Bad, horrific, times do happen. We can't hold them back, but we can plant the seeds of the future. I think that is the sacred therapy for surviving catastrophes. Etty Hillesum (1914–1943), in the year she was murdered at Auschwitz, reminded us: *"And, if we just care enough for each other, God is in safe hands with us, despite everything…"*

A friend, on being diagnosed with a fatal illness, went directly home and helped her granddaughter with her homework. No matter what the disaster, God is in safe hands with us if we just care enough for each other.

January 19
The Spiritual Experience

Rainer Maria Rilke (1875–1926) wrote: *"God is not a destination but a direction."*

Whatever our story, there is a common desire for nourishment and comfort. Perhaps we may have felt that in our youth, but it may not be there in the same way now. No matter what our stories have been, you and I are often on the same path. We may be coming from different directions, but at some point your experience meets mine.

Historically I come out of a Catholic heritage. These days I personally don't find much in common with the official Roman Catholic Church institution. But I think the heritage is rich, and the Vatican doesn't own it—it belongs to everyone who wants to be a part of it. In the same way, I have no trouble in respectfully borrowing from Buddhist, Jewish, Protestant, Native American, or any other spiritual heritage.

Even if we have trouble defining the term "God," we know what Rilke was trying to say. Spiritual growth is a progression unique in every person. I personally don't believe

there is any place for dogma or creed in the process —
only experience.

Onward.

January 20
From the Hands of
Every Child

I would like to reverse a familiar phrase in use and say – *"It takes a child to make a village!"* In every newborn child lies our planetary hope for the future. We all belong to him or her just as she or he belongs to all of us. In these times, the miracle of a new life unites us.

During a long life, it is easy to lose track of what is important. Money, position, careers, honors, ideologies, and esteem are completely without interest to the newborn. He sees things I have forgotten: the shadow on the wall; the spider finding a hiding place in the rocks. She hears the soft distant call of birds, of the wind. She looks really deeply into the eyes of the cat; she values warmth. Every moment of life is celebrated!

I think this is what the Buddhists mean by "mindfulness." We all had it, but may have dropped some important things along the long path of life. That's OK. The baby is coming on the same path and picks up these things we let fall, and hands them back to us at an age when we really need them.

January 21
Yield and Overcome

I know a man who searched all over the world for a sense of wholeness. He had been a teacher, a missionary in Africa, and desperately followed many other paths, only to reach spiritual dead ends.

Finally, he came to a monastery with the thought that those men must know how to reach God if anyone does. For years he tried hard, but his sense of emptiness increased. One winter day the community was pruning its extensive fruit orchard. Mountains of cuttings were piled at the end of the row. It was this man's task to take the cuttings to the pile. All day he worked at this monotonous task. Then, the sad thought occurred to him that the job resembled his spiritual life where, day after day, he did the same thing, over and over, without getting any closer to an experience of the sacred. In that melancholy instant, he accepted defeat and gave up his lifelong quest.

As he reached for the next branch, his hand and the dead branch became one. It was as if a patient universe had been waiting for the door to open and now came pouring into the man, filling him with great joy and peace. In that moment he knew himself, God, and everything else.

January 22
On a Rainy Day

A frustrated cat sits on the windowsill watching the rain. His plans for the day are being washed away — and so are mine.

Maybe our lives are like drops of rain. There is beauty and joy in being a single drop. It is exciting to fall. Each drop reflects beautifully all the colors of the rainbow. However, there is also weariness in being so individual and fragile and having to contend with time and space.

Perhaps there will come a time when, like a raindrop, we will each lose our separateness and merge into a pool of water. All that is each of us will come into a complete stillness.

Well, it's a thought at least. The cat has gone to sleep by the fire — that is another idea.

January 23
The Story of the Land

Those who share the land on which I live work to maintain our land as a sacred spot in an increasingly threatened landscape.

Over half our farm is forested. This will remain foreverwild. The area where we live, grow olives, garden and harvest fruit has been under cultivation for over a century. Before that, it included a clear hillside where Native American Peoples came to dry food for the winter. And before that, it was where the ocean touched the land.

We know we are part of a long story and have an obligation to be good stewards in our time. In turn, the land, as it goes through the cycles of growth, helps us comprehend and experience the cycles of our existence.

Wherever you live, you are also part of a long story.

January 24
The Song of the
Fisherman

There are many references to *"the song of the fisherman"* in Chinese stories. Although the beginnings of the fables vary, the endings are usually the same: a famous statesman is found on the riverbank by the emperor's envoys. They bring news of his appointment as prime minister. He interrupts the formalities with *"Listen! The song of the fisherman,"* drawing attention to an ordinary man downstream.

Through the centuries many weary pilgrims have used the simple song of a fisherman to mitigate the complexity of life. The poet Wang Wei (699–759) wrote:

As I grow old, I only want peace.
Affairs of the world no longer rouse my tired heart.
I go back to my house in the woods.
The wind blows through the pines and caresses my clothes.
In the mountain moonlight I play my lute.

You ask if I have yet produced a philosophy
to explain life...
Listen! The fisherman's song floats on the river.

January 25
The Promise of New Buds

Next to the path between our house and the chapel was an old apple tree. It had been there much longer than I have lived here. It came down in an early January storm. Later, we will cut up what remains for firewood, and it will give us warmth and a sweet smell. This too is part of nature's story.

January can be hard. It can also be a gentle time. Within the starkness of the landscape I find the first small buds on the remaining apple trees. Someplace deep in the woods an impatient wild plum blossom opens a bit. And for an old man, there will still be fresh moments of life. The taste of an apple is in the breeze.

But for now, it is starting to rain. Being by the fire is also a reality, a blessing of this month. Brew some tea. Remember and dream.

January 26
A Patch of Blue Above
the Clouds

We all have doubts about our ability to encounter the sacred within our human experience. These are holy doubts. No one has the answer to our questions. It is frightening to have only our own meager resources standing alone before a sometimes demoniac army of problems, suspicions and fears. It is a battle we will never be able to win.

One day, however, we may find a little patch of blue sky above the battle clouds. It is said that the Buddha would walk up to his intellectually troubled disciples and hand them a little flower. In the fight with demons, Evagrius Ponticus (345–399), a Christian desert monk, advised; *"Do not fight them, jump over them!"* Is it still possible in our sophisticated age to transcend our oppressive concerns, to jump over our demons, and to accept the little flower?

I suspect every one of us knows that we each must, at least once, have the courage to try.

January 27
Warriors of
the Rainbow

The Book of Genesis says the rainbow is a sign of the covenant between God and humans and *"every living creature of every kind that is found on the earth."* A great many of the first peoples of this continent also have the rainbow in their creation stories. They are all different, but many of them fall into a pattern. There was harmony in the world and places of tranquility. Then the "invaders" — our European ancestors — came and broke this circle of peace. These invaders were people of greed and fear and violence.

But the story is not over. A prophetess of the Cree Nation had a vision that the earth would be ravaged and polluted, the streams poisoned, the birds would fall from the sky and then "The Warriors of the Rainbow" would come to renew the earth. And, very like Jesus' *Sermon on the Mount*, the poor, sick and needy would be once again cared for. As the Oglala Lakota Sioux chief Luther Standing Bear (1868–1939) put it, *"all things that were, will be again."* The Hopi think it may be even better,

> *When the earth is dying*
> *there will arise a new tribe*
> *of all colors and all creeds.*

January 28
Learning the Dance of Life

When I am holding my infant grandson, Damien, and something startling happens, he looks at me to see if everything is alright. Thus we share ourselves and our values with our children.

Fashioning the way in which a person and a society lives a wholesome and happy life is an ongoing quest. I think God left it largely to each generation to figure it all out for its time.

It is reasonable to look to our religious traditions, but there is often a problem about how this wisdom is presented to our children. If it is overly harsh and rigid, it is ineffective and counterproductive.

Rather than dogmas, we need to learn the steps in the dance of life that can be used in meeting both difficult situations and ordinary living.

January 29
My Poem, Your Poem

Many years ago I attended a poetry reading by a friend, Robert Duncan (*1919–1988.*) After he read, a young person reacted to a poem. Robert asked, "What did you hear?" After listening carefully to the response, Robert said, "That's beautiful. It is not my poem. It is your poem—and it is good."

The encounter between Robert and the young person is how our joint quest for finding the sacred in life should unfold. The world in which we live is in serious need of spiritual refreshing. Let us each treasure our ideas and our contributions. Martin Buber (1878–1965) wrote that a spiritual encounter is *"going to meet that which is coming to meet you."* It is a good concept.

January 30
Both Ways are Right
Ways

In the late 1960s, when my own spiritual community was forming, two of us accepted an invitation to visit the Shakers of Sabbathday Lake, Maine.

One evening, we were sitting around the great stove in the Sabbathday Lake kitchen. Sister Frances had baked gingerbread from an old recipe. This led us into a discussion of other treasures from the past. I had been reluctant to mention that we sang their hymns. I thought they might consider it presumptuous of non-Shakers. When I did tell them, they wholeheartedly approved of our doing it.

Eighty-year-old Sister Mildred promptly asked us to name a favorite and to sing it. We sang *'Tis The Gift To Be Simple.* When we finished, we asked if we were doing it the right way.

"Oh, yes," said Sister Mildred, "you sing it the right way." The other sisters nodded and smiled. I was amazed we had sung it properly.

Sensing my thoughts, Sister Frances said, "We sing it a different way, but both ways are the right way."

January 31
A Time to Plant

On the farm where I live, it is the time for planting trees and bushes. New roses can be enjoyed in a year or so. But fruit trees are another matter. A lot of care is taken in digging the hole, spreading the bare roots, covering them, and gently pressing or watering out open pockets below the surface.

I am at an age that I am now helping to plant trees whose fruit I may not ever eat. It seems a common ritual in advancing years — the business of working for a future you may not share. I think of my parents, who likely had the same experience.

I pat down the earth around a new tree more than is really needed. I use it as an excuse for appreciating the tree and anticipating the future. All through life it is important to plant without concern for future personal enjoyment. A person cannot really be whole without contributing in some way to the common good.

In recent years, there has been a long overdue rush to take better care of our planet. Most people around me

are quite serious about attempting to reverse the conse-
quences of our past exploitations. Some things probably
cannot be reversed for centuries. But this is a season for
making what amends we can.

FEBRUARY

FEBRUARY 1
A WINTER STORM

Some days are really bad days. I am told that in early Japanese poetry the word *kogarashi* (often translated as *withering* or *winter* wind) was unique to the winter season and connoted a powerful force strong enough to break branches. Obviously no one can control this *Winter Wind*. Think of every place there is war, human-trafficking, poverty, hunger.

Hopefully there will be solutions — but not today. That is one image to keep in mind. But here is another, a plain, authentic, solitary person selling simple food — perhaps soup, or a burrito, or a cup of coffee. Issa (1763–1828) brings these two images together in a haiku:

As the winter-wind crashes above,
someone is selling soup below.

Today, could you or I be that someone?

FEBRUARY 2
CANDLEMAS

Today is the mid-point between the Winter Solstice and the Spring Equinox. From very ancient times it has been the beginning of the farming season. Long ago church authorities converted this day into a feast of light, when candles are blessed, but the real commemoration is still to be found outdoors.

Around me, right on cue, the camellias and the daffodils are blooming. This is that special "ordinary time" that is free of the expectations of Advent-Christmas and Lent-Easter-Passover. In the country, we hear tractors. In the city, we hear traffic. But still, looking at the tiny yellow flower of some scrawny weed, there comes an inner quiet that helps us face really significant questions like, "What is my life all about?" As we get older that question shifts into the sometimes more desperate concern for finding or fashioning an environment "where we may live a worthy life."

So here we are, we who gaze at a candle, a blossom, a weed, opening ourselves to a wordless and unexplainable wisdom helping us discover where, and how, we may live worthy lives. A lot of people have stood where we stand. On an ordinary day. A wonderful ordinary day.

FEBRUARY 3
PRAYING WITH AN OWL

The night is cold. The sky is clear. I am sitting comfortably inside musing on the year ahead for me, those I love, the planet I inhabit. Suddenly there is a loud thump on the window behind me. Out on the deck is a slightly dazed young owl who quickly regains his composure and gracefully flies away.

As I watch, the thought comes to me that owls, monks, aging folks all have something in common. We have opportunities to pray for the world. I don't mean, "Lord forgive all these awful sinners who surround me." But we pray on behalf of all the other folks who are taking their rest and who will make the world go around when the day breaks.

Do owls pray? Of course they do! As do all creatures who bring authenticity to the earth by simply being themselves.

Tall redwoods and Douglas firs surround me. But beyond these shadows I sense the almost empty city streets, the hospital corridors, the refugee camps, mothers creatively distracting hungry children, the sick and lonely wondering about the wisdom of going on, the young, eager to claim their heritage, all types of lovers escaping over the walls of self-absorption.

For a moment, just by breathing in and breathing out, I feel in spiritual solidarity with all others; past, present, future.

February 4
When the Day is Gray

There are not many leaves on the branches of the trees around me. The sky is a little grayer. And in my hand is a letter from someone who has experienced a great loss and asks, "How do you handle grief?" What do I respond?

My friend, I know you hurt. I would like to simply sit with you and watch the birds but many miles separate us and words will have to do.

Yours is a question that demands an honest answer and I have to say, I don't think I do handle grief well, I simply live with it.

I was born long ago and have encountered so much death and new life that, frankly, it all seems to run together. At emotionally shattering times I do find strength and comfort in a number of things, most especially faith and peace.

I have a strong faith but I can seldom make sense of it. My intellectual understanding of mysteries such as "God" is constantly changing. Regardless of that unsatisfied curiosity, I somehow comprehend that life has meaning. I cannot truly walk long with anyone who wants to capture the sacred in a box. But I do find companionship with all who seek for transcendence even though their experiences are different from mine.

Peace often comes down not to words but empathy — not to beliefs but to hugs. I'm satisfied that something divine is in there somewhere. And around us there are birds — and silence – and the smell of apple blossoms – and also a pain in the heart.

FEBRUARY 5
TO LIVE LIFE AS IF IT
REALLY MATTERED

Sometimes it seems as if there is a universal uneasiness about how we use the gift of life. Could it have something to do with a confusion about the purpose of that gift?

Those of us old enough to have suffered through catechism classes would have memorized something like, "*God made me to know him, to love him, and to serve him in this world and to be happy with him forever in the next.*" I think that is way off the mark. There was an alternative "New Catechism," which had a brief existence before it was expunged, where it was suggested that the first step in understanding the Gospel's "Good News" was "*to live life as if it really mattered.*" Other people have come to the same conclusion and it makes a lot of sense to me.

But doesn't everyone live life as if it matters? I don't think so. In fact, we are pretty good at distracting ourselves from facing that issue. What is a person's distraction of choice—money, prestige, drugs, alcohol, life in the fast lane? How about always being Number 1? Never settling for anything but the best? Always being right, and on the "right side?" Being in that number when the Saints go marching in? Or a fruitless striving for perfection?

Living life as if it mattered means, among other things, accepting our imperfection. It means we simply do the best we can. Occasionally, rejoicing in the fact that we are simply another human being at this moment in a long history. And, at the same time realizing that we do matter — we are each a necessary note in a beautiful song.

FEBRUARY 6
OUR TASK IS TO BE

If everyone has a task, what is mine? What divine instructions have been implanted in my spiritual genes? The millions of words I have read, heard, thought, and written, in the end, can be reduced to a few lines from the prophet Micah (6:8):

This is what Yahweh asks of you—only this:
to act justly,
to love tenderly,
and to walk humbly with your God.

Just that. Nothing more.

FEBRUARY 7
THE HEART OF A STAR

Out on the Kalahari Desert, I am told, a mother still takes her newborn out on a moonless night and holds the baby up to the sky, asking that her child's heart be exchanged for the heart of one of the billions of stars she sees about her. These are people who have not forgotten how to listen to the stars, and the mother goes away confident that her request has been granted.

Primitive silliness? Today, scientists say everything has been made of stardust. That would include your heart and my heart.

FEBRUARY 8
WHEN EXPERIENCES BLEND

L istening to a string quartet, I realized that what they were doing would never be duplicated. The story of each person playing, from birth till now, was being poured into the music as they encountered the story of the composer's life. I was hearing those stories. There was a child near me listening, and perhaps her story was also going into the mix of that magnificent experience.

At home, the olive trees will soon begin to blossom. Each one has a unique structure. I believe that there is something in this diversity that is essential for the wonderful oil that is produced.

Just as with the musicians and the olive trees, differences often help produce the richest results.

February 9
Life and Death are One Thread

Death is a name we give the act of returning. Only our individuality has a limited existence. In only a few months a sunflower will sprout, grow, bloom and produce seed. When the great stock withers, turns brown and falls to the ground, we say that it is dead. But nothing in nature can really cease to exist.

Last year I was watching some sunflowers grow, bloom, produce seeds for the future. The large stalk withered, turned brown, and fell to the ground. The sunflower had performed its mission. Then it returned to its source. As it did so, it nourished other parts of the great community of life. What remained of the sunflower became quiet and after a while merged with the ground again. Perhaps it will remain in the quiet forever, or it may again be used for another of life's stories. A number of elements were brought out of their quiet to produce what we have labeled "sunflower." Now it has returned to its source.

The saga of every living thing follows the same course. We all come from a common quiet, become a unique individual part of creation and, at death, return to the commonness.

February 10
After the Peak

A signal that we are approaching a fundamental change in our society is the large number of people who look outside our culture for a balanced way of life. For all its greatness, western civilization seems fragile.

> *"Whatever has been forced to a peak of vigor,"* cautions Chapter 55 of the TAO TE CHING, *"approaches its decay."*

We have made it a goal to operate at a "peak of vigor." It is not surprising that we may be approaching decay. This is one deep and inescapable rhythm in history. The TAO also counsels us that: *"Movement overcomes cold, stillness overcomes heat."* (Chapter 45).

Is our society becoming so hot that more and more people are getting burned? Every moment of stillness contributes to a better balance.

February 11
Blessed are the Curious

In the middle of the 20th Century, I joined many people in the Western world who had a growing spiritual yearning and looked eastward for comfort. It was an exciting time of experimentation. We tended to move with fascination from one spiritual import to another. It was fun, but sometimes shallow. I often found myself playacting. I bought a meditation pillow and imagined myself a Japanese Zen Buddhist. Attracted to the serenity and wisdom of Tibetan teachers, I wondered if I had not known them in some earlier existence. At various times I was also pretending to be a Hopi, a Sufi, and a Shaker.

But after a few months with each new discipline, there was an inevitable awkwardness, and I had to separate adventure from authentic experience. My inner needs were never satisfied by attempting to import spirituality from a different cultural environment. Some people are able to transcend their backgrounds, but many of us are not.

However, when we can graft our cross-cultural spiritual experiences on to our own cultural roots, we should be very grateful.

FEBRUARY 12
EDUCATING THE HEART

Aristotle (384–222 BCE) warned, *"Educating the mind without educating the heart is no education at all."*

Every child is naturally awed if he or she is in an environment that does not take everything for granted and one in which the adults are willing to admit that they do not know everything. One of the most important memories that people consistently recall as they attempt to reconstruct their spiritual history is the awe of being alone or with a loved adult in a special and holy place.

We must educate children to expect the unexpected and be open to it ourselves.

Hermann Hess (1877 -1962) urged us to find Holy ground within each of us. What about prayer? Hesse said we should just sing forth our suffering, our joys, our thanks – "as little children sing."

February 13
Spiritual Generosity

If I can be a person for others and find God in others as well as in myself, then I can dance around the universe with another human being.

It is a relationship I cannot control. I am vulnerable, and perhaps afraid, as I encounter someone who is encountering me. However, as a result, I lose my separateness and become more fully human.

It is the most nourishing and authentic encounter I can have with another person--and also with God.

FEBRUARY 14
ST. VALENTINE'S DAY

It probably all began with a poem Geoffrey Chaucer (1340?-1400) wrote to honor the English king and queen.

For this was on Saint Valentine's Day
When every bird comes here to choose his mate.

The first problem is birds in England don't generally mate in mid-February. It is too cold. Secondly, there are several St. Valentines and it is likely none of them had anything to do with lovers. Some of these "saints" may not have existed at all.

But February 14th was assigned to one St. Valentine, and so we have the day, and I like it. Besides, some birds in California are mating!

Valentine's Day need not be only about florists, candy-makers, and greeting card manufacturers. For young and old in love it is an excuse for a tender touching. Should someone haul out a red tablecloth and suggest a candlelit dinner, I am right there. Especially in times of stress, I welcome any ploy for expressing love.

FEBRUARY 15
INVESTING IN THE FUTURE

I have a friend named Mike. He was recently asked to speak to a group of professional and business people about his spiritual journey. A former District Attorney and soccer coach, Mike is known for getting right to the core point. He entitled the brief talk *"What Do I Tell My Grandchildren?"* That is an interesting and worthwhile way to look back over the path we have each traveled, and forward to the young people in our lives. He ended the talk with his answer to the question in the title:

"I don't tell them anything — it is what I DO that's important!"

Mike is right. And, that is the hardest part of being a guide to those who will inherit this planet.

FEBRUARY 16
ALONG THE PATH

Walking the Way of Jesus is the only means of understanding him. The starting point for us has to do with the realities of life in our age. Some recurring themes today harm both individual and community life. There are different opinions on what all these issues are but most lists would include a reference to the growing selfishness and the resulting loneliness.

Does the experience of the followers of Jesus have anything to contribute to that issue? Yes. The same could be said of the followers of Buddha, Muhammad, or any other religious leader. They are all needed, for there is an urgent necessity to encourage the development of a global ethical perspective-- a common ground for how we relate to each other.

Part of Jesus' approach was to serve as a host at meals for those who, for various reasons, were not welcome at most respectable tables. Eating and drinking with his friends and social outcasts was a very inclusive style of life. Jesus encouraged people and made them happy.

Like ourselves, Jesus was in a process of realizing the potential of his personhood, which included merging the divine and the human. In a more limited but nonetheless deeply significant way, each of us has been invited to merge those same elements in ourselves.

FEBRUARY 17
DEEP IN THE COUNTRY

Basho (1644–1694) was probably resting under a tree and listening to farm women, ankle deep in water, singing as they planted the rice seedlings when he wrote a famous haiku,

The beginning of culture deep in the country a simple rice planting song

I don't hear that in my rural California home. Out here, it is agribusiness, and the planting is by giant noisy machines. Perhaps what I call "noise" is the beginning of our culture. However, there are also flocks of birds calling to each other as they explore the turned- over earth. I would like to take their songs as the beginning of our culture.

No rice here either. Mud and plum blossoms are the February realities where I live. So where is the sacredness? In the mud? In the blossom? Could it be in both?

FEBRUARY 18
THE EAR OF THE HEART

Some days I think all that is required of me is to be truly quiet. If I do that, maybe everything else I want will happen without any effort. The willow has only to stand still and the wind will move its branches. If the willow tried to create a wind by frantically waving its branches it would miss the real wind when it came. I know that my attempts to create a wind can quickly exhaust me.

St. Benedict (c 480–547) in his instructions to monastics says we should *"listen with the ear of your heart."* It seems to me all my life my heart has been singing a song I never quite hear. But sometimes, in a rare moment of stillness, it somehow touches and refreshes me.

Perhaps, at times, that is all that is necessary.

February 19
Thoughts On Looking
At A Candle

Leave the hot wax in the hollow at the top of the candle and it is fuel for the flame; spill the wax and it makes splotches that are difficult to remove.

We are all born with an inner force. When we release this strength for external things, like gaining, mastering, competing and possessing, it is quickly used up. When the force is left to develop in the quiet emptiness of your inner being, it grows and grows.

At times of spiritual fatigue, we are all given the opportunity to plug the holes through which our strength has spilled out. I often find myself plugging those holes in the beauty and silence of nature. But everyone has a place where they can go to feel peace and gather their strength.

Whatever it takes, let us allow the light within us to brighten.

February 20
A Blessing Of Rain

We live in a society that is overscheduled, overcommitted, overextended — and we like it that way! If a moment opens up in our lives, it does not present a peaceful opportunity for reflection or awareness, but rather a space to be filled. A Silicon Valley psychologist suggests that we have an absolute fear of slowing down. And I will admit that I sometimes feel this anxiety myself — when in doubt, check my iPhone, otherwise I could miss something, or, even more serious, I could be bored!

I like the attitude behind what is sometimes called "Buddhist Lent." It takes place in the weeks of rain. Buddhist monks and other contemplative folk take shelter and reflect, retreating inside and letting nature prepare itself for new life.

It rains here in February — sometimes for days or weeks on end. It is easy to get bored with the gray days and itch for a little sunshine. It is harder to accept this time for what it is — a time to reflect, to sit around the table with family, to watch the fire dance, to listen to the rain. To rest, as nature does, before the explosion of life and activity that comes with spring.

FEBRUARY 21
A PLACE NEARBY

The medieval pilgrimage was very popular, and it is becoming so again, being much more convenient with jet travel and comfortable hotels in Jerusalem, Mecca, Lourdes, El Camino de Santiago, Kyoto. But how can people fly off when they are young and have a child to take care of and must struggle with all the challenges of living? Or when they are old, and have difficulty making ends meet or simply coping with life?

I have been to a lot of pilgrimage sites in my life. On a recent birthday, I was given a wind chime. It hangs on a crabapple tree which is just beginning to bloom. There is a gentle breeze blowing. I am going to walk out to the tree and listen to the chimes. At this time in my life that is my pilgrimage-of-choice. We all have such a place.

February 22
Gaining Strength

Sometimes the only satisfying path leads us into a storm. There are practice sessions for those times.

Lent, the time leading up to Easter, often begins in late February. When I was a child, around me the birds might be busy and flowers could be appearing. But behind church doors was a parallel universe. Sister Muriel, my sixth grade teacher, would ask us what we were giving up for Lent. We would try to outdo each other in proclaiming our fervor.

I have learned self-denial is a tricky business. It usually makes sense only if it is part of something else. Giving up sleep to watch the beauty of the dawn is part of an increased awareness of the sacredness around us. Avoiding activities that distract us from looking at ourselves, or our world, also makes sense. A pregnant friend checks her e-mail only once a week. She wants to focus on bringing a new life into the world.

Much of nature gains strength by surviving adversity. Fruit trees must endure many hours of winter chill to ever produce. Is denial for the sake of toughening up us humans also justified? The Islamic world fasts from dawn to dusk during the month of Ramadan, a practice that is really hard for Muslim kids in American schools. But they learn more about what is truly essential and the beauty of a simple life.

FEBRUARY 23
DIPPING INTO
WALDEN POND

This is a good time of year to make our lives more spiritually healthy. That will mean many different things for different people. Some practices are very simple. For example, with all our WI-FI technology it is getting harder to "unplug" from the world and experience the quiet facets of life. So, looking on Henry David Thoreau (1817–1862) and his life at Walden Pond as a sort of golden age of simple living, writer William Powers recommends "Walden Zones" in our lives.

"Walden Baskets" for cell phones have been popping up with people around me. It does feel good to drop my phone into a basket when I leave the house and walk to the chapel or greenhouse. And, you know what? The world keeps on turning!

February 24
What will Make my Spirit Grow?

On a beauteous day at the Shaker Village in Sabbathday Lake, Maine, the Meeting House was full. Many personal and societal woes were being shared.

Suddenly a young Shaker across from me stood up and said, "Why all these words? We all know love is the cure!" Then in a pure voice she led us in this simple Shaker Hymn: *Love is little, love is low / Love will make my spirit grow. / Grow in peace, grow in light / Love will do the thing that's right.*

In these spring days, let us be open to what is little and low, confident that love will always enable us to do the thing that's right!

February 25
Hope: Psychologist,
Pope, Author

This season is changing in the world around us. Is something also happening in our inner world at this time?

Many years ago I asked the psychologist Carl Rogers (1902–1987), a person whose opinions I valued, what was the greatest problem that he thought we would face in the future. Without any hesitation, he answered, "*The increasingly rapid rate of change.*"

Much later, a new pope, Francis (1936-) said there is a universal "*nervousness and self- absorption.*" I think Rogers' and Francis' thinking go together. So what do we do about it? Is there any hope for a way out of this?

I know of no wiser advice about that "*fleeting and threatened*" hope than what Albert Camus (1913–1960) said, before either Rogers or Francis, in his Uppsala lecture:

Create dangerously: ... Some will say that this hope lies in a nation; others in an individual. I believe rather that it is awakened, revived, nourished by millions of solitary persons whose deeds and works every day negate frontiers and the crudest implications of history. As a result, there shines forth fleetingly the ever threatened truth that each and every human being, on the foundation of his or her own sufferings and joys, builds for all.

That means you, me, and every other human being we encounter today.

FEBRUARY 26
GOING OUT AND
COMING IN

Walking can be a prayer. Walt Whitman (1819–1892) was described by contemporaries as someone who was always *"going out and coming in."* That is more or less what the Zen Buddhist teacher Thich Nhat Hanh (1926 -) means by *"Walking Meditation."* Have these two people simply hit upon a way of avoiding reality in our challenging world? No. Whitman served as a nurse to the wounded, broken, and dying in Civil War hospitals. Thich Nhat Hanh is a peace activist and was a delegate to the Paris Peace Talks in 1969 that were preliminary to ending the Vietnam War (December 1956-April 1975.) He speaks of *"Engaged Buddhism"* and reminds his followers that the Buddha did not stay sitting under the Bodhi Tree after enlightenment but got up and spent his life walking the troublesome roads of the world.

Over the years, I have come to the opinion that *"going out and coming in"* would be a beneficial aspect to my spiritual life. I walk with slow, little steps, often in harmony with my breathing. I am not going anywhere, simply rejoicing in the journey — like a young child, or as a Navajo blessing puts it:

With beauty before me I walk. With beauty behind me I walk. With beauty beneath me I walk. With beauty above me I walk. With beauty all around me I walk.

February 27
Lessons from a Plum Tree and a Mountain

The first blossoms of any fruit tree make poets of us all. Yet, spring blooming is only possible because of the stark period of winter dormancy. Also, the lush summer foliage will begin to die back as the energy of the tree is directed toward the fruit which contains the seeds necessary to secure the future of the species. After the fruit is harvested, the dying leaves provide a breathtaking splash of red, orange, yellow and brown upon the landscape.

We, like many ancients, can study the fruit tree to discover ways in which we can better harmonize with life. Many Asian spiritual teachers see in the annual natural cycle a mutual interdependence of two necessary life forces; "YIN" (quiet, receptive, reflective, earthy) and "YANG" (active, bright, assertive, expanding horizons.) It was assumed that for the healthy life, of both the individual and society, Yin and Yang must merge together. They are the two sides of a mountain, as one sage put it. There cannot be only one side of a mountain — or of a life.

FEBRUARY 28
THE SONG OF LIFE

The older I grow, the more I learn from musicians, poets, artists, and others who move outside the rational box in which we attempt to confine our spirit.

There are healing and refreshing songs in each of us, in our history, environment, relationships, dreams, and prayers. The Hopi people in Arizona sing:

And the bird's song, and the people's song, and the song of life, will all become one.

It is true, and in this song of life, we each have notes to sing.

February 29
The Added Day

Every four years, usually, we put some left-over time into an extra day. In this way we keep earth time aligned with the revolution around the sun. A Caesar named Julius (100–44 BCE) thought this up, and it appealed to the Roman sense of order. No one has explained this to the hummingbird drinking at the fountain, or the plum tree in blossom, or for that matter to the millions of humans who think of the year in terms of moons and not traveling around the sun. To the farmers following the Farmers' Almanac we are someplace in between the "Full snow moon" and the "Full worm moon." Jewish calendars have leap months seven times in a 19-year cycle. And so it goes.

Today, if we wish, we can forget about Julius and others obsessed with keeping time precise. There are many days in our personal life that do not fit in any calendar. The day a friend died. The day a child is born. The day we received some very bad or very good news. The day our life changed. The day the world changed. Many days when 24 hours were not enough to experience what was happening.

Today, if we wish, we can take a holiday from time. It can be a timeless day. A day to just be. Like the hummingbird and the plum tree.

MARCH

MARCH 1
YIELDING AND SIMPLE

Walking on a stormy day, I see how the many trees around me respond to the wind. I can't help feeling that every life has those storms and, like the trees, we must react. How?

Many sacred writings, from different places on the spiritual spectrum, warn that rigid trees break in a tempest but flexible trees survive.

Chapter 76 of The Tao cautions:

> ... *the stiff and hard are attendants of death, the supple and soft are attendants of life.*

An old Shaker Hymn puts it plainly:

> *Yielding and simple may I be, like a pliant willow tree.*

Good advice for doing the best we can in unsettling times.

MARCH 2
AS THE EARTH AWAKENS

One of the great miracles of March is something I will probably never personally experience — yet I think of it often. In New England, when the nights are cold enough to freeze and the days warm enough to thaw, the sap of the maple trees begins to flow. The Native Americans discovered this and it didn't take the new people from Europe long to catch on.

The slow-growing maple tree will not be hurried. The season is short and the process laborious but the rewards are wonderful. My family does a little trading with friends — California olive oil for Maine maple syrup.

Equally gratifying is the awareness that the sap is rising all around me. The world in which we live is alive. And that can be happening in each of us as well. The vitality of our spirits is being renewed.

This is March — a symbol of sweet balance – in the maple tree, and hopefully in each of us.

MARCH 3
WILD OATS

Walking around our farm, I discover little patches of tall wild oats. They're not supposed to be here. In the 19th century, they covered this county. A friend tells me that a farmer coming from Missouri wrote in his diary "that the wild oats grew tall enough to hide a man on horseback." Then came decades of clearing the land for farms, cities, roads, vineyards, resorts, and all the rest that the civilized world brought with it. The wild oats were gone — but they aren't.

Millions of good people have lived their lives the best they could. And, like the wild oats, they left seeds in our seemingly barren and meaningless spiritual landscape. But just like the wild oats, those seeds can sprout and grow again in surprising places.

I think that is happening now. Young people who no longer feel themselves trapped by oppressive religious doctrine and culture are frequently among the first to find spiritual sprouts surrounding ordinary lives. Where did they come from? It doesn't matter. They will be very valuable to our unfolding future. No matter what our age, that is exciting to contemplate!

MARCH 4
PRAYING FOR A RAINY DAY

As I grow older I sometimes become less enthusiastic for the cycles of nature, or of life, to change. But they do, no matter how I feel about it, and I know that.

There is a prayer-without-words that spontaneously seems to arise in me at times of change. It comes from my fear of not being able to cope with things that will come and my sadness at letting go of the place where I have been resting.

Though almost bloomed out the flower raises its head to the morning sun.

Have you ever wished for a rainy day when others are playing and stretching in the sunshine? I have. Spring is here — but first, could I not have one more cup of tea, while sitting by the fire with my cat, and listening to the rain?

March 5
Is The Future in
My Hands?

Could it be that all the beautiful things in life have their beginnings in the earth? These days I am surrounded by seed catalogs and have been planning this year's garden. It is an important annual ritual. I choose the plants I know from experience to be reliable in our area. And, with small cautious steps, I also venture into the unknown.

As I gamble on choosing the right variety of corn this year, hoping to erase the memory of last year's fiasco, I also find my thoughts drifting to the seeds of our human race. How will the toddler at my knee grow? How will the child leaning against another grandparent's leg, halfway across the world, grow? What will happen when they meet each other twenty-something years from now? It is unlikely that I will ever know. I would be 104+ by then. Nonetheless, I feel that other unknown grandparent and I have some responsibility to prepare for such a meeting.

Just as with the garden seeds, the future begins now!

March 6
A Silent Song On A Gentle Breeze

Some days I just cannot figure out what to do. How to solve a problem. What to do about the distress of someone I love. The loss of someone or something that means a lot to me. The last thing in the world that occurs to me is just to be still and quiet. But that is often what is needed.

It is hard to trust that the wind of some silent song will touch, refresh, and heal us. Could it be that all my life my heart has been singing a little soundless song which is part of the great silent song of life itself?

Could it also be that the birds singing around me know more about this than I do? If I am still, will that song my heart yearns for be carried to me on some gentle breeze? Do I have any better ideas? Not at the moment!

March 7
Plant A Seed

M any, many years ago I heard some ancient wisdom. The language was old-fashioned and not inclusive, but somehow it struck home for me. It went something like this:

You must plant seeds.

Plant your seed now. Not tomorrow but today! Let it grow. In a few days you will learn what to do next. You must never neglect your plant for even a day.

Sometimes you will plant new seeds. There will be times for gentle pruning and times for daring transplants.

Be aware, alert, and vital. Respond to what you hear and see.

When I remember this advice, I find myself more in harmony with heaven and earth.

MARCH 8
ROOTS AND BRANCHES

Our spiritual roots intertwine with the roots of trees. Occasionally this is quite dramatic. Siddhartha found enlightenment under an ancient fig tree and became the Buddha. Jesus spent the most difficult and agonizing hour of his life surrounded by old olive trees.

Annually, Jewish communities celebrate *Tu B'Shevat*, a new year for trees. Perhaps this is why Israel is one of the few countries on our planet with more trees at the end of a year than at the beginning.

Our challenges in life may not always correspond to the seasons of the year, but sometimes they do. Like trees, we have times of bareness when we are hit by storms —what Emily Dickinson (1830–1886) called an "Hour of Lead." At these times we may lose hope.

The trees around us go through a cycle every year. There is wisdom and strength to be found in slowly walking among them at any season. But in the spring we can become aware of a symphony of hope. Soon there is a bud. Then come beautiful flowers and smells. On bare branches, tiny new life begins.

MARCH 9
BACKYARD PILGIMAGE

The seeker-as-pilgrim has a long history. My friend Paul Clasper (1923 – 2011) called the pilgrim a person questing for *"the real heart of all authentic living."*

I think Paul was saying that the successful conclusion of any pilgrimage is to find our authentic self. I think that was going through the mind of the poet Issa as well (1763–1828). Where he lived were seven very impressive temples dedicated to seven deities. When the first crabapple blossoms appeared, the local custom for his neighbors was to spend the night visiting the seven temples and participating in elaborate ceremonies.

But, where was Issa? In his yard was a rustic post his father had erected for some forgotten reason. As Issa's neighbors were in the streets going from temple to temple he wrote,

On this chilly night, my Temple Pilgrimage is to this little backyard post.

MARCH 10
HAVE I BEEN ME?

In his *Tales of the Hasidism*, Martin Buber (1878–1965) has a poignant story.

A rabbi named Zuzya died and went to stand before the judgment seat of God. As he waited for God to appear, he grew nervous thinking about his life and how little he had done. He began to imagine that God was going to ask him, "Why weren't you Moses or why weren't you Solomon or why weren't you David?" But when God appeared, the rabbi was surprised. God simply asked, "Why weren't you Zuzya?"

I can imagine Buber's God patiently sighing and saying, *"I didn't need another Moses, or Solomon, I needed you."* So should we ask how we have been at being ourselves?

MARCH 11
AS THE SOUL GROWS YOUNGER

Oscar Wilde (1854–1900), and others I think, said, *The soul is born old but grows young.* So how do we experience the soul growing younger as we cope with shuffling around the aging process? Composers have sometimes introduced the hurdy-gurdy man at this juncture of body and soul. In *Winterreise,* Franz Schubert (1797–1828) had a deeply disappointed person encounter this "curious old fellow," and together they walked off singing and playing their song as best they could.

It has been said that as we grow older we are, if we so choose, better able to hear the music that has lain quietly in our souls. And we become more aware of those moments when it is very important to sing our song.

Perhaps that is the lesson to be learned. We just sing our song as best we can, and hopefully in that process our soul grows younger!

MARCH 12
HOPE FROM LITTLE THINGS

One of my oldest friends was a beloved public official who fought successfully for better government and better care for all citizens. Now in her retirement, she finds herself with very serious mobility issues. Recently she wrote to me, *I saw myself as the one always helping people with disabilities, never thinking the day might come when I needed help!*

I am sure that sounds familiar to many of us. So what keeps us going? From whence comes our hope? The same friend wrote at another time,

> *There is a continuous miracle of plants surviving in spite of all odds. My poinsettia which was small and everyone thought was dead has now spouted three new leaves on one tiny limb among all the "dead" limbs. I kept watering and talking and praying for a miracle, and so far, so good!! It is the little things that give us hope and pleasure!*

Truly, it really is the little things that give us strength and hope — and pleasure.

MARCH 13
WHAT HAD TO MOVE
MOVED

Teresa was a "good girl" who grew up in a church family. She did well in school. In college, she began to really explore beliefs and life on her own. Church faded from her priority list. She looked for nourishing relationships with ethically responsible people. Right after college she married and began a promising career in education. She had done all the things she was supposed to do. However, her husband drank too much and his eye roamed too much. The dream of early motherhood evaporated, as did her career, after the 2008 financial recession caused cuts in school budgets. Now she is struggling to make ends meet. She finds herself a recipient in a food pantry where she previously had been a donor.

What weighs on Teresa most heavily is that she cannot answer the question, "Why me?" She asks the unknown and mysterious cosmos, "What did I do wrong?" It is very hard for Teresa, and most of us, to accept that the answer is sometimes "Nothing." 1000 streams come together to meet at every moment we are living! We have very little control over them.

So is there anything we can hold onto in bad times? I think it helps to realize that whatever has happened is not all about me or you. We are each part of a big story. We are all leaves on the tree of life – and sometimes leaves fall.

MARCH 14
A WAY TO WALK

I am deeply troubled by many of the statements from those who claim to speak for Jesus of Nazareth. Yet I have spent much of my life crudely stumbling along the Way of Jesus as I have perceived it. So I am a Christian, and it seems to me that as Christians willing to explore our role in the scheme of things, we should begin not with the Church, or Christ, or even God. It would be more authentic to start with what it means to be human.

Through our awareness of ourselves and of the sacred dimension in life, we could help counteract the constant tendency to slip into a shallow existence. I sense this is the path Jesus took. Christians are at our best have been when we encouraged each other to live life more fully — as if it really mattered.

March 15
Justice Works for God
And For Us

When I was very young, we had to memorize many things as we made our way along the stepping stones to promised salvation in the Catholic Church. One task was to recite the Corporal Works of Mercy. After reciting them to the catechism teacher, we would receive a star on the proper line of our progress chart. Then most of us probably put them out of mind. That was unfortunate, because they are good spiritual guidelines if we really live by them.

Jesus frequently echoed an attitude from the Book of Isaiah (58:6–11) where an exasperated God let it be known he had no interest whatsoever in people covering themselves with sackcloth and ashes, moping about, and fasting. Forget all that stuff. What works for God is for people: to break unjust fetters and undo the thongs of the yoke, to let the oppressed go free, and break every yoke, to share your bread with the hungry, and shelter the homeless poor, to clothe the person you see to be naked and not turn from your own kin…. If you do away with the yoke, the clenched fist, the wicked word, if you give your bread to the hungry, and relief to the oppressed, your light will rise in the darkness, and your shadows become like noon. Yahweh will always guide you, giving you relief in desert places.

If we want to encounter the divine element in our lives, we must develop a compassionate response to our brothers and sisters, which is, in turn, a way of recognizing that we are dependent on each other to find relief in desert places.

March 16
A Place To Hold Hands

Our first association with a spiritual group is usually not a matter of choice. But all other decisions, including remaining or returning to the community of our childhood, should be a deliberate choice. Spiritual companionship may be as simple as the fellowship of one other person or as formal as active parish membership. There are many factors which lead each of us to seek a spiritual home in a particular environment.

In finding a community, I think it wise to remember Andre Gide's (1869–1951) advice: Believe those who are seeking the truth. Doubt those who find it. The relationship is nourishing only if it provides a bridge from our individual life experience to the reality of global existence. The community should not limit our view of human existence, but stretch us to expand our horizons.

A spiritual circle of choice should help us find common ground with others who differ from us. We must accept the necessity, and hopefully see the advisability, of divergent approaches peacefully living side by side.

MARCH 17
SAINT PATRICK'S DAY

It is said everyone is Irish today, unless of course you are gay and trying to get into the St. Patrick's Day Parade in New York City. Well, it turns out that Patrick wasn't Irish. Probably he was born and raised in a part of Britain under Roman control. Everything about him is a bit hazy, but the story goes that when he was about 16 he was captured by Irish raiders and taken as a slave to Ireland where he lived for six years before escaping and returning to his family. Later,

probably in France, he became a Christian and joined up with the church of Rome. At some point he returned to Ireland as a missionary bishop.

There are a lot of myths surrounding this fellow. For example, it is said that Patrick drove the snakes out of Ireland but it turns out there never have been any snakes in Ireland. Oh well, just order another Guinness and Sláinte!

But, there is one thing that has always fascinated me. A long Irish prayer has been labeled "St. Patrick's Breastplate." It was the spiritual armor he wore when, like a Roman legionnaire, he was going into Religious battle. He clothes himself in all the traditional beliefs and dogma of the church of that time. But in the middle of it there is an extremely interesting verse which I believe probably went back to more ancient times:

I bind to myself today: The power of heaven; The light of the Sun; The brightness of the moon; The splendor of fire; The flashing of lightning; The swiftness of wind; The depth of sea; The stability of earth; The compactness of rocks.

Sometimes when we are in the midst of a powerful emotional, spiritual, or physical struggle it is good to look beyond the battlefield and to remember these things. Maybe Patrick didn't compose this prayer but somebody did, and as we all know — today everybody is Irish!

March 18
A Song of the Earth

Where I live in the country, there is now a strong feeling of newness and anticipation. It is refreshing to become aware of so much new life. In the blackberry bushes, a squadron of quail are born — each with a little top feather. They follow jerkily behind their parents out upon the meadow, like a line of marching commas. Bees come from nowhere and search out pollen. Tiny wildflowers appear everywhere. When the sun sets, the frogs signal their presence with an alternating chorus of sound and silence.

Rachel Carson (1907–1964) once wrote, "Those who contemplate the beauty of the earth find reserves of strength that will endure as long as life lasts." It is easy to agree with her on days like these!

MARCH 19
SAINT JOSEPH'S DAY

In medieval illuminations of March, especially in southern Europe, activities are portrayed which I can also observe around me today on neighboring farms and vineyards — plowing, pruning grapevines and fruit trees, planting.

This is a time to remember an ordinary father and husband who had to handle some extraordinary challenges. In parts of Italy people have long identified with Joseph – "Giuseppe" – as someone who understood the plight of the common man and woman. In some places, where special foods are prepared this day, bread crumbs are incorporated to represent the sawdust in Joseph's carpentry workshop. There would also have been also curls of shavings which no doubt became the playthings of Jesus and his siblings.

Like Joseph's shavings, these are all signs of hope, the expectations of ordinary folks living close to the land. Many of us in sunny climates also have a wish that any depression and sadness descending on us in the winter months will now blow away. Or, at least we will experience an emotional balance as we are surrounded by signs of new life and vigor.

As he began his workday, perhaps Joseph would have sung what the Psalmist wrote long ago, "*This is the day the Lord has made, let us rejoice and be glad!* (Ps 118).

MARCH 20
THE NOW OF SPRING

Every year is a four-act improvisational play. There is no rehearsal. There is no re-take. There is only NOW, and we do the best we can. We live in that "Eternal Now" as Christian mystics termed it centuries ago. Or as Henry David Thoreau (1817–1862) put it:

> *You must live in the present, launch yourself on every wave, find your eternity in each moment. Fools stand on their island of opportunities and look toward another land. There is no other land; there is no other life but this.*

Around us nature is changing from the dormant to new life. We open ourselves to the freshness of new life, nature's reminder for us to live NOW.

MARCH 21
AN EQUAL DAY IN SPRING

I love those lines from the *Song of Songs* (2: 11–13),

For see, winter is past, the rains are over and gone. The flowers appear on the earth. The season of glad songs has come, the cooing of the turtle dove is heard in our land.

The vernal equinox is a natural time for an international celebration. Day and night are equal everywhere on the planet. There is a moment when the sun crosses the equator. Ancient observatories were established to verify the day and the moment at Stonehenge in Britain, Mayan Pyramids in Mexico, Temples in Egypt, among the pueblos of the Southwest, in the jungles of Cambodia, on the mountains of China and in most other cultures.

This was a big-time day! It has continued in many places. Europe has Spring Day on the 21st when bells are rung. In Japan, it is a day to appreciate nature and visit graves. For Afghans, Bengalis, Tamil and followers of Bahá'í and Zoroastrian faiths, it is the New Year. For South Africans it is Human Rights Day. In many Arab countries, it is Mother's Day. Egypt has *Sham el-Nessim* meaning "smelling the breeze." And they go out into the country and do that! Easter is set on the first Sunday following the first full moon after the vernal equinox. Each year, at the exact moment of equinox, the Peace Bell is rung at the UN in New York.

This is a time for the human family to celebrate our diversity and our harmony — starting with you and with me, and the flowers appearing on the earth!

MARCH 22
A NEW SEASON, AN
OLD BLESSING

A few times each season my family stands quietly on a hillside and slowly surveys the land we are privileged to inhabit.

To the north is the unchanging and quiet forest, growing unattended. Facing east, where the sun rises, we remember new beginnings — birth and hope. In the full, warm sunlight of the south, we carry out most of our daily activities. Here the land bursts forth with fruit. Turning to the west, we recall the many times we have watched the sun set and understood the harvest-time of each season and life.

There remain two more directions. At our feet is the tiny patch of earth that is our home. Here, for us, the mystery of life crosses the path of history. This is where we live. This is where we find the face of God in a tiny wildflower.

Lastly, if we are fortunate, we can watch a bird fly up into the sky and hopefully, in some way, each of us feels the divine and unchanging spark within us. Probably, from the earliest of times, people have been doing the same thing.

March 23
Where We Are,
Who We Are

The lessons of spring are bursting out all around us. This season will pass quickly. It is hardly the time to think ahead to our final days. Or is it?

Considering our death has at least two quite different benefits. One is practical: making sure we have a will, a durable health-care power of attorney, discussing our wishes with those we will leave. But there is something else which is even more important.

Reflecting on our final hours can give us a perspective on how we should be living our life in the present moment. Looking ahead, and then turning around to look at where I am now, helps me see more clearly what is important and what should be skipped over.

March 24
Above Dry Fields

Once, stuck in a wheelchair, watching apple blossoms drift down, I became rather depressed. There seemed no way for me to participate in the freshness of the season.

Late in his life Basho (1644–1694) wrote,

> *Taken ill on a journey but still my dreams roam over the dried up fields.*

When we are caught in some kind of cage, old or sick, and frustrated by what we can no longer do, our dreams really can be as lively as ever. Now Spring surrounds us, and we may feel sad not being able to dance with the wind in the trees — but our dreams can.

Where do our dreams take us? Time can evaporate. All the Springs of our life can be in this present now-moment.

MARCH 25
WHAT HAPPENED?

Quests for authenticity sometimes take us into deep and uncomfortable places and at other times we may soar. I am in my 80s and frequently ponder the meaning of life but my friends in their twenties are also asking, *"What is my purpose in life?"*

I read of a young graduate from an Ivy League university who said in her freshman year she never met anyone who wanted to be a banker, but at her graduation there was a fifty percent chance she would be sitting next to one. Making gobs of money in the financial world had replaced their earlier dreams.

It is tempting to suggest that people think of what they will be proud of in their final day of life.

In time most of us will have lived through a lot of personal and societal changing experiences and become well aware of the provisional nature of human existence. Given all that, it is still good to ask ourselves, young and old, the same questions – *What do I choose to be my purpose in life? What do I want from life? What was my dream? What was my passion? What happened? What now?*

MARCH 26
AN OPEN QUESTION

My sister Marti had a theory that those like me, born just as the Great Depression was ending, are part of what she called "the warhorse generation." Hearing of a problem we react like a racehorse hearing the bell, and just charge down the track. She may be right. I know of a number of friends in the birth-class of 1931 who would fit that description! But surely even warhorses get to retire to an idyllic pasture. Right?

Does our responsibility for the future stop at some time? I have done my bit and now I have other things I have to consider; physical and emotional problems, losses and grief, desires for simple moments, for peaceful times to watch a butterfly or listen to a Beethoven symphony. And any other grandparent in a faraway time zone would, I am confident, have similar challenges and desires.

Did I hear a bell?

MARCH 27
I CAN'T GO ON. I WILL GO ON

R ecently I read something by a 36-year-old surgeon who had just learned, in fact read his own CT scans, that his cancer had widely metastasized. What to do now? Prepare to die? He is terminally ill, but in some ways we all are. Mortality is something we eventually have to accept, especially when spurred on by aging or CT scans. So what to do now? This young physician remembered a few words from Samuel Beckett (1906–1989), he had read years before when an undergraduate, "I can't go on. I'll go on."

The doctor wrote that the alarm goes off every morning and he thinks – I can't go on – and then he is in his scrubs, heading to the operating room and he knows – I'll go on.

Well that is how it ought to work, in one way or another, for all of us. My friend, the psychotherapist, Elizabeth Bugental (1926–2009) put it very straight,

We grow daily, as we die.

March 28
A Pew Among The Trees

Why do questing people still go to Church, Synagogue, Zendo? There are many reasons, perhaps the strongest is to have the support of a spiritual community. For others, the search takes them beyond support. They're looking for a touchstone, a core, an answer to, *"What is my life all about?"* Or they may want that mysterious yet necessary experience of the transcendent by being in a sacred space.

However, some serious seekers may feel out of place sitting in a pew with satisfied folks who are attending because it makes them feel good, or it is a habit, or they like the music, the pretty vestments, or the sense of a weekly hour of specialness.

So if that doesn't fit you, where do you go? Well, there are those like Wendell Berry (1934 -): *I go among the trees and sit still. / All my stirring becomes quiet around me like circles on water.*

We all have special places where it seems the pieces of life's puzzle fit together. The trees. A view. A gravesite. A gazebo. A garden. A chapel. Those reading these words could add many additional places. All of them are sacred.

March 29
Lesssons From A
Double Feature

In those long-ago days of my childhood, the Saturday afternoon double feature was part of my ritual of life. I only rarely got in at the beginning of one of the movies. It did not seem to matter to any of us to be there when it started. At some point I would say, and it was always the same phrase, *"This is where I came in"* and I would make my way down the row, into the aisle, then out into the bright sunshine of reality.

My life has frequently been an exploration of something new. Born in the late Depression, then the world turned upside down by World War II, the post-war prosperity, the struggle for civil rights and liberties, the redefinition of what it meant to be a human being, new frontiers in the inner world and spiritual life. So it has gone for all of us plus major challenges in family and personal life, and health, and aging.

As my life unfolds, I do sometimes think *"This is where I came in."* I just hope that what is happening is my following those lines of T.S. Eliot (1988–1965) in *Little Gidding*,

> *We shall not cease from exploration And the end of all our exploring Will be to arrive where we started And know the place for the first time.*

MARCH 30
PRAYER?

In Asia, when people have tried to touch the spiritual essence of existence, it has frequently been by listening. In the Western world, it has most generally been by talking. There have been some exceptions. The Danish theologian Soren Kierkegaard (1813–1855) wrote, *"The function of prayer is not to influence God, but rather to change the nature of the one who prays."*

An increased sense of wholeness comes whenever we try to touch some sacred space in our lives, our society, or our history. These efforts are not always labeled as "prayer," but that is what they are. Teresa of Avila (1515–1582) compared praying to watering a garden. Sometimes we have to carry buckets from a well, and this can be burdensome. At other times, it is possible to design and use an irrigation system. Sometimes it simply rains, and we don't have to do anything.

"Prayer" for me is any attempt to experience the divine element in our lives, any awareness of the presence of God, any longing to find peace in the depths of our being and in the world where we live.

March 31
Being Open to New Horizons

As our spiritual horizons expand, we see the same subjects but with new eyes. The process requires an interaction between several evolving circumstances. We are usually aware of our changing personal attitudes. We experience the point of view associated with infancy, school age, adolescence, youth, maturity, old age. Our attitudes about almost any subject are going to grow and develop as our life unfolds.

When there is a retardation of growth, problems will occur. The same thing can happen spiritually. We can freeze at a school-age concept of a God who can help us pass an English test, win a basketball game or open a stuck locker.

Normally, however, our concepts mature as we age. But personal development is not the only factor involved in our expanding horizons. Our civilization is not static but is also in a maturation process. The state of our common knowledge is constantly changing. The spiritual attitudes of a people before Darwin's concept of human evolution were quite different from those following that discovery. We are now, post-Darwin, in the next phase of this ongoing evolutionary process. As the French paleontologist, philosopher, and priest, Pierre Teilhard de Chardin (1881–1955) put it some time ago, *We are the universe become conscious of itself.*

Another horizon. Another rise in our mindfulness of what it means to be alive, our relation to other living things, and our quests for the sacred.

HOLY WEEK

A WEEK MADE HOLY

Sometime between the middle of March and the middle of April will come the Jewish feast of Passover and the Christian Holy Week. Traditionally Holy Week is organized something like a Mozart concerto. Palm Sunday is the first movement — *allegro,* a joyful celebration. But everyone knows that at the end of the week we will have the second movement, what Emily Dickinson (1830–1886) has called *"The hour of lead."* Then the next Sunday, Easter, we move beyond joyful — *allegro con brio!* Are those enough performance notes for you?

Some poets suggest that this week is an allegory for reinvigoration after devastation. For myself, I am attracted to the theme and rhythm of walking. There was a lot of walking. The crowd walked down the hillside waving branches and welcoming Jesus like a breath of fresh air. I have walked those steps, as well as the steps on the streets where tradition says he walked to his execution. And I have walked to the ornate church which many say enshrines the empty tomb.

I feel it is important for me this week to keep on walking. It's not as easy for me as it once was and I appreciate companions. One group are those close to me — human friends and animals who know well the land on which I live. Another is made up of the many I do not know who are trying to make their lives and this world a better place. Let us be "Mothers of God" as Meister Eckhart (1260–1328) put it, *"we are all meant to be the Mothers of God, for God is always needing to be born,"* and reborn in our age.

And so, making peaceful steps, we move on to a Holy Week.

PALM SUNDAY

On this day, throngs of Christians around the world will be walking in solemn processions, waving palms or olive branches, and shouting "Hosanna." The political theater being acted out when Jesus entered Jerusalem centuries ago was a precursor of conflicts that have remained with us to the present day.

It was Passover and hundreds of thousands of Jews from all over the Roman Empire had come together to celebrate at the Temple in Jerusalem. The Romans were control freaks and saw enormous challenges to their oppressive rule in such crowds of freedom-loving Jews. So up from their comfortable city on the Mediterranean came the Roman governor, Pontius Pilate, and a large cohort of soldiers and cavalry. Real Hollywood stuff meant to intimidate the populace: horses, armor, military formations, trumpets, drums, lots of metal and gold — power, power, power. Entering the western gate, their presence proclaimed the Roman Empire and the Emperor Tiberius, who was the stepson of a god.

Then at the same time entering from the eastern gate comes a rag-tag peasant mob with Jesus riding on a donkey. What were those ordinary folks proclaiming? The

Kingdom of God, not Rome, symbolized by telling the Passover story of God's deliverance of the Jewish people from slavery in Egypt. Probably there were people following Jesus who didn't know much about him but were simply in favor of anything that was not Roman.

Which procession would we have been in then? Now?

MONDAY IN HOLY WEEK

It is important not to over-indulge in somber Lenten rituals. True to her blunt-speaking Jewish heritage, St. Teresa of Avila (1515–1582) put it well in a prayer, *"From sad faced saints, O Lord deliver us!"* Jesus would have recently participated in the joyful Jewish spring festival of Purim and heard read out from the Book of Esther, *"For the Jews there was light and gladness, joy and honor."*

At my home we let the apple trees guide us to an awareness of the "light and gladness" that is around us. Those trees are also symbols of reinvigoration. Sitting under the sweet smelling branches of an ancient tree recently, I jotted down some of what I saw and heard — shadows of honey bees on my paper, apple blossoms drifting on my shoulders, finches singing, a dog running Carmen-like with an apple branch in her mouth, a cat wide-eyed on a branch, a blanket of tiny purple flowers leading from the tree to the chapel.

I find it takes courage to respond to the apple tree's invitation to join the spiritual dance celebrating new growth. I don't do it well. But I try. And, as with any prayer or meditation, the doing and the trying are pretty much the same thing. Wherever you are, and whatever around you brings a fresh start to mind — will you join in the dance?

Tuesday in Holy Week

S ometime this Holy Week most of the Christian world will hear a powerful statement from the Hebrew Bible. *"Redress the wronged, hear the orphan's plea and defend the widow!"* (Isaiah 1:17)

There are a lot of terrible things happening on our planet. Each of us has different situations that hold our attention when we hear about them or see something in the paper or on TV. What hits you hard? I know for me personally it usually has to do with a young child looking up at an adult who might guide him or her out of a horrible situation. On my desk is a picture I clipped out of something. It shows a woman with three children walking along the railroad tracks at Auschwitz. The children are following her with confidence as they always have. She knows this is the last time.

I recently saw something just as powerful filmed in Syria at night using that eerie green light. The young boy, about eight years-old, is in a group attempting to escape into Lebanon. He is looking at his young mother for direction. That boy's face is one I cannot get out of my mind. We are told his father had been stopped at the Syrian checkpoint and shot. This Muslim mother is trudging onwards exactly like the Jewish mother in the 70-year-old picture on my desk. Will it never stop?

The Catholic biblical scholar Carroll Stuhlmueller (1923–1994) wrote that those words from Isaiah *"symbolize in the Bible all the helpless and indigent people of the world."* So what do we do? It begins by not averting our eyes or attention from an unpleasant situation right in front of us!

WEDNESDAY IN HOLY WEEK

Mid-week. Some things accomplished. Still much to do. But this being Holy Week it is important to leave a little space for awe. There are many wonderful moments in this day, as in every day. One is when night becomes day. Hans Küng (1928 -), one of the most respected theologians of our age, wrote, "*What tranquility and grandeur the starry heavens radiate... so I reflect again on the great questions the cosmos puts to human beings ....*" One Holy Week I asked some friends to react to that. These are a few of the simple experiences they shared,

I am in awe when I go out in the dark morning to retrieve the paper. The air is still, the world is asleep, and there is a peace that transcends all for those few minutes. I think that when I retire, I will go outside just before dawn to sit and reflect as the world awakens around me. ... Every morning I get up before dawn, walk outside to ponder my garden, and with gratitude notice the beauty and potential of the day to come. How I love the night sky!! ... From my childhood I remember sitting on our back porch and just gazing at the moon and stars. ... Last night I opened the door and looked up into the night sky. ... So calming, so grand, so radiant. In an instant my perspective changed and all became right

*in my world. ... Tonight I am going to stop trying to make
sense of the world and just sit under the stars. ...*

And now, perhaps before the Milky Way fades, it is time
to open the door, take a deep breath, and "reflect again
on the great questions the cosmos puts to human beings."

HOLY THURSDAY

Christians often call the meal on the night before Jesus was murdered the "Last Supper." However, there were no Christians at that meal. They were all Jews because this was the Passover feast — the Seder. But they weren't all the same kind of Jews. One of them had even cut a deal with the police to help arrest Jesus! Around that table were people with many different beliefs and doubts and lifestyles. That was the point as Jesus gathered together his extended family in preparation for his saying farewell. Everybody had a place at the table, no one was excluded. As *The Didache*, a First Century Eucharistic prayer put it,

> *As different grains have been gathered from the hills and baked into one bread so may your people be gathered from the ends of the earth…*

There is much I have taken from that Passover meal in Jerusalem centuries ago. It echoes to the present day. I will never forget Tammy, a nine-year-old girl dying of AIDS, saying to those of us in her room on the last day of her life, *"Remember me at the parties!"* I cannot help but believe that was partly what was in Jesus's heart that night as his companions sang and danced to celebrate the Passover from slavery to freedom.

Someday it is going to be the time for each of us to leave something to those we love. What will it be?

GOOD FRIDAY

Today we remember Jesus' execution centuries ago in Roman occupied Jerusalem, and also all the points in everyone's life when we experience what Emily Dickinson (1830–1886) called, *"The Hour of Lead."* That hour is still ticking away all around us. The words of a couple of people are much with me on Good Friday.

Dietrich Bonhoeffer (1906–1945) was a German pastor at the center of Protestant resistance to the Nazis. He was arrested and later hanged less than a week before the Allies reached the prison.

> *The Bible directs us to God's powerlessness and suffering; only the suffering God can help us. ... The world's coming of age has done away with a false concept of God and opens up a way of seeing the God of the Bible, who achieves a place and power in the world by his weakness.*

It is in our shared humanity and weakness that I feel most in solidarity with Jesus of Nazareth.

I also think of Issa's (1763–1828) poem:

A bug on a branch swept away down the river still singing its song.

We may be on our way to ruin, but even in the "Hour of Lead" we must still sing our song!

Holy Saturday

This is a day for taking a breath, but it is not simply an emotional transition between Good Friday and Easter Sunday. There is a question or two we could be thinking about today.

Paul Clasper (1923–2011) was a good friend. In 1950, Paul and his wife were appointed Baptist missionaries in Burma both of his daughters were born there. Later, he was Anglican Dean of St. John's Cathedral in Hong Kong. Paul always considered himself a missionary no matter where he was. But his definition of the task of a missionary might trouble any Christians who would attempt to put the Way of Jesus into doctrines and rigid boxes. Paul said, *"My job as a missionary is to discover how God is breaking through in cultures other than my own."*

Today is a good day to ask ourselves, "How is God breaking through in cultures outside our comfort zone?" And what if that breakthrough is a still and quiet process?

In my lifetime, organized murder of the helpless was a prized skill. Hitler and accomplices slaughtered over 20 million non-combatants. 62 million dissidents died in Stalin's reign and a like number under Mao. Today as I

140

write there are 51 million refugees in the world from conflicts in the Middle-East. And what of the young who die in
gang warfare? On and on, it does not stop. How does God
break through in cultures of death?

Perhaps a partial answer was found scrawled on the walls
of a cave near Cologne where some French Jews were hiding from the Nazi terror:

*I believe in the sun even though it is late in rising. I believe in love
even though it is absent around me. God is silent yet I do believe.*

This is perhaps an age when God may be silent in order to
help us listen to our own hearts.

Easter Sunday

Today we gathered before dawn around a little fire. Then we lit a candle and carried it into the dark chapel for a gentle service. We came out as the dawn was breaking. It was one of those moments when I could feel the entire community of existence and was glad to be a part of it!

There was awareness of everything around me –

Apple blossoms on the old tree. Rusty antique plows. The huge spruce tree we light on Christmas Eve. The sound of the gravel on the path. The cats and dogs playing around. The big brass bell brought to us from China by a ship's captain. The lavender plants. And looking up, I see on the distant hills the redwood forests. The giant trees seem to accompany me down the hill. I sense old friends who were here long before me. A carpet of wildflowers. And the peaceful, graceful, olive trees dancing in the morning breeze. The awakening birds. Everything, including my heart, is heralding the season of new life.

How Jesus came to be still existing among us after his cruel execution I do not know, nor care. What I do know is that death was not the final word for him. And I also know that today there are many other folks out there on many paths. We are all united in some way. Watched over by these towering trees and made happy by the flowers around us.

APRIL

April 1

An Apple Blossom Day

Like quiet snowflakes the white apple blossoms drift on the April breeze.

There is something very special about an apple tree in April. We can smell the blossoms and almost hear songs on the breeze. Where I live, we go to the chapel sometimes and share haiku- like moments we have experienced under the branches of an apple tree.

In these days of battling theologies, it is important to remember that the simplest aspects of nature can provide nourishing common ground. Ellen Gould White (1827–1948) founded a very conservative Protestant denomination. She observed, *"God is Love is written upon every opening bud!"* The Catholic novelist Flannery O'Conner (1925–1964) wrote things like, *"... he saw Jesus move from tree to tree in the back of his mind, a wild ragged figure..."* And, the beloved Emily Dickinson (1830–1886) gave the apple tree the place of honor in her Amherst garden. From her upstairs window, she watched the sad corteges of the young killed in our Civil War pass in front of her house. For Emily and for many of us, apple blossoms make a healing balm.

April 2
Finding The Balance

Generations of Asian poets and painters have known the necessity of a refreshing place between our inner experience and the outer world. I have come to agree that grace and beauty are preconditions for my spiritual health. An ancient school of thought suggested that beauty had something to do with "harmony," a word whose Greek roots mean "fitting together."

There are countless ways of moving toward harmony. Each thought suggests several others: nature, gardening, cooking, watching the steam rise from a cup of tea or a funky corn dog, children, a home, looking at a pine cone, experiencing the seasons, poetry, art, music, walking, swimming, dancing, a ritual.

What we experience is a balance between many things: what is known and what is unknown, the natural and the cultivated, the moving and the still. Out of such experiences come the healing and inspiration that is essential for our spiritual vitality.

April 3
The Little Things Are Important In Life

Saint David of Wales lived in the sixth century. The story is that his unwed mother had been raped by marauders. She gave birth to David on a cliff during a violent storm. David's life continued to be rough, but he founded many monasteries. Before a great battle he taught Welch warriors to wear leeks on their helmets. Well they won, and Welch soldiers have worn leeks into battle ever since!

Anyway David did a lot of things and lived to be over 100, which makes his last words to his followers all the more touching to me,

Be joyful... and do the little things that you have seen me do.

Saint David was also a great bee-keeper. For an old fellow like me there is something very special about the buds bursting into blossoms. I will never hand out leeks to soldiers, nor have a great spiritual following, but I can watch the bees fly from blossom to blossom. And remember there is something forever young and fresh within every little thing — including me and you.

147

APRIL 4
WHEN I LOSE MY WAY

On the path to the greenhouse, garden, orchard or even chapel, I am often concerned about how vulnerable I am in facing some unwelcome challenge. Or maybe it's not about me, but about a friend, or even the whole society around me. I'm in a fog. I lose my direction. Which way do I go? Where is that damn compass – that face of God?

Then I start to look around. In the early light of a new day, the bees are awakening, a butterfly is on the lavender. The personal story I am struggling with co-exists in this moment with a story as old as the first lavender plant, bee, butterfly. Perhaps as old as the first dawn. My concerns are real but they, and I, are part of something bigger.

The compass I long for is always near me. A Hopi farmer would call it "The Song of Life". All our struggles enrich that very long song, and it helps carry us through our trouble in life. And the whole song carries me through the bad patches of my short-term personal struggles.

Something sacred is always breaking through in our stories, even though the times may be rough.

April 5
Judging The Day

It is tempting to try to control every step of our lives. But if a good farmer feels a desire to raise corn, he or she does not wait for someone else to supply the corn crop. The farmer plants a kernel of corn, and devotes attention to that piece of corn. As the kernel sprouts and grows the farmer learns from it what next to do.

Robert Louis Stevenson (1850–1894) wrote, *"Don't judge each day by the harvest you reap, but by the seeds that you plant."*

Today, let us all walk quietly at some point along the silent paths of our inner gardens. Eventually we will hopefully enter a nowness where there is no time. In that moment, we will feel at home, and one with all of life. It is then that we should listen, really listen. We will feel our destiny quietly unfurling along our garden paths.

Once we have a sense of direction, then we must go and find a seed to plant. In this way we can each be creators and builders.

April 6
A Simple Harmony

Albert Camus (1913–1960) once said something to the effect that happiness was the harmony between ourselves and the life we lead. And, I think, the essence of harmonious living is to prefer the simple path to the twisted.

Living the simple life means moving into nature's house. It means never losing the sense of awe for our host and yet always feeling at home. It is good to learn to value what is natural.

To live simply is to breathe in unison with the day. Everything that comes to us is a gift. May we discover the grace to use it well!

APRIL 7
WHICH WAY? WHICH WAY?

D o you every feel spiritually lost? Or even lost in general? I do, and I think everyone has times in their lives when they lose their way. At those times, we all wander. It is lonely. And each step seems to take us farther away from a nourishing path.

When that happens, it is easy to end up frantically thrashing around in the wilderness. To forget the spiritual path and go off seeking money, respect, knowledge, power or some other means of privilege. We do this only because we are holding on to the one thought that possesses us—how to stop that dull, constant heartache. Not finding a way to do so, we may then want to just give up.

But I promise you, there are simpler ways to live. If we can just stop trying to find a ladder that will reach the sky, perhaps we will realize that the sky will come down to touch us.

APRIL 8
SPECIAL PLACES

Many folks I admire find their special place, their Sabbath spot, in a circle of trees. Probably the place I feel most at home is in our little chapel. Our first one at Starcross was a Native American teepee donated and set up by a friend. Next, the chapel was in the hayloft of the 1902 barn, just above where we milked the cows at that time. We would sing and they would moo!

But one summer the barn burned down. Then, we built the present little six-sided chapel on the hill that separates where we live and farm from the area that is dedicated to be forever wild.

So many important and moving events have happened in those sacred spots. But when I sit in the chapel and think back over the years, it's a few little violets and weeds that make up the bouquet that stays in my mind.

We all know there are many things wrong with our world. Some serious things which seem to be getting worse. Those are all part of the big story. But we mustn't let them destroy the little violets and weeds: the smile of a stranger;

the laugh of a child; the hand of a friend; the trust of an animal. The breath of peace in a prayer.

Where are you most at home?

April 9
Letting Go And
Becoming Connected

Detachment is one of those big items in spiritual growth. It is taught by many world religions as one of the greatest ways to achieve peace. But in the beginning, the process of detachment can seem cold. When a person sits in meditation or prays by resting in the hands of God, she empties herself of everything. How lonely that sounds. But being alone is not necessarily lonely.

To detach from our preoccupations is to have faith in the life process and to know that we are a part of it. Through detachment we do not forsake people and our environment. Detachment is a means of connecting with them at a deeper level. For it is not people or things that distract us, but our desires. It is from these desires that we must learn to detach.

Detachment begins by entering into the silence of your own inner being. There is some kind of a spark there. We have to adjust and become aware of it. For a moment we can be searching for nothing else. We are letting go and at the same time becoming connected to all that is.

April 10
Knowing Me

O ld Aristotle (384–322 BC) wrote, *"Knowing yourself is the beginning of all wisdom."* But how exactly do we go about doing that?

There is a rich experience around each of us and "inside" each of us. Today is as good a day as any to recognize, or remember, that each of us is a rich experience, and it is necessary to become aware of this experience.

For me it starts by not asking, "What does it mean?" To ask that is to set ourselves an impossible task. The object of self-exploration is not to analyze, but to hear. Once a person asked a composer to explain a musical composition. The composer looked at him and said *"Listen to it again."* I try to remember that. Exploring my inner world is not an analytical exercise but something to listen to – over and over again.

It is easy to get frustrated with not finding answers. "Why?" and "What?" and things like that. But when we become more and more aware we most likely are already experiencing changes in the process of knowing ourselves. And that wisdom gives us clues about what to do next!

APRIL 11
IN AND OUT. IN AND OUT

The Zen monk and peace activist Thich Nhat Hanh (1926-), who is more or less of my generation, said that feelings come and go but breathing can be an anchor. As I get older, I've learned to appreciate each breath that I'm able to take. In and out. In and out...

Every breath really is a cycle of life, a season in itself: we take in the sweet spring, we fill up our lungs with the summer, we experience the autumn joy of letting go and then become empty and still in the winter. Now we can breathe again, for there is always a new beginning and a new ending.

I've gone through many seasons of my life and have learned that we, each of us, will never take a breath more or less important than the one we are taking now. We will never be in a day or year more or less important than the one we are in now.

It's good to remember that every single breath is a new beginning of life.

April 12
Letting Go

Dying is not separate from living. Our lives can actually prepare us for dying, just as our death can assist us in life. The full realization that we will all someday die can actually sharpen our awareness of what it means to live.

It seems to me, at times, we live in an age quite bent upon denying our mortality. If it were possible we would make 80 "the new" 20! That is unfortunate because we cut ourselves off from the wisdom that comes from accepting the fact death will come to each of us. As the progressive theologian Karl Rahner (1904–1984) put it, *"Death contains within itself all the mysteries of human life."*

It is not easy to let go of anything. Certainly not life itself. But as numerous poets have written, when we do let go we often make room for love.

April 13
The Cave Or The Frontier?

The poet Robert Duncan (1919–1988) was a wonderful friend. Of all the things Robert wrote and said one is forever etched in my mind,

"Every moment of life is an attempt to come to life."

I have been hurt in life. You have been hurt. Our family, country, culture has been hurt. And, after any hurt, it is always difficult to take risks again. We want safety and security. We find threats, enemies, dangers all around us.

Somehow we must continually find the courage to risk, because it is by taking risks that we free the great creative energy within each of us.

Learning to live with uncertainty is a life-long lesson; we should quit trying to distinguish between what is certain and uncertain. If our ancestors had not done that we would still be living in caves.

There will be hard times but living with uncertainty calls forth our strength and our vitality. It is really important to live on our own frontiers.

APRIL 14
LIFE WITHOUT UMBRELLAS

When a child was in the hospital and I was almost paralyzed with fear, this thought came to me from nowhere,

"Think of the petals of a daisy."

So I did. The daisy has no extra coat for a cold night, no umbrella for a hot day. Such protections would weigh the petals down and eventually bend it away from the rest of the flower. Then there would be loneliness and feelings of being different and inadequate. It would do no good to add more overcoats and umbrellas; the extra weight would only make the problem worse.

Shedding all of our neatly created protections is uncomfortable. We often feel exposed when we drop our baggage. It's just so tempting to save a little something—just in case!

But don't do it. In order to truly see what is around us, to really feel our own strength, we must stand alone in the desert. Then we will finally see that we are already at home.

The child? She recovered and then she had a use for my strength, not my weakness. Think of the petals of a daisy!

APRIL 15
ME OR MY MASK?

The disciplines of spiritual growth are often demanding. Its rewards are not always immediate. So why do it?

If a person is not committed to his or her own growth, there is no reason to undertake this journey. If we are committed, then we explore our inner worlds simply because it is a necessary part of all of us.

It's not always easy to be ourselves. Ralph Waldo Emerson (1803–1882) wrote that the world was constantly trying to make us be someone else. That is often true, and we must be able to really hear what is going on with us. The masks we wear for the benefit of others often deceive us as well.

The Book of Proverbs wisely tells us we must drink from our own well — be it bitter or sweet. If we want to change or grow, we have to accept where we are and be who we are.

April 16
My Note, Your Note

Hey, I know the answer to the big question: what is the meaning of life? It is life itself, the song of life! And it would not be the same song if we were not each there to sing our note!

Once standing outside in line to enter a theatrical performance a young woman came up to me and said, "I just wanted to thank you for saying something that saved my life." Then she disappeared into the crowd. I had no recollection of having met her before. Perhaps we passed each other on a train platform, or sat next to each other in a coffee shop. But somehow I seem to have sung my little note when it mattered to her.

Arid times are going to come to each us and to those we love. We need to focus on the song that surrounds us. Each of us is truly a necessary part of that song. It may be a glorious solo or one simple note at the proper time. But each of us is needed. And we have to keep reminding each other of that!

APRIL 17
NEW ROADS TO PEACE

I heard someone ask an Islamic Latino why he, raised as a Catholic, became a Muslim. He hesitated a minute and then said with a smile, "Peace." I could understand that and I thought of a Middle-Eastern woman I know who, raised Muslim, joined a Catholic community for the same reason.

Probably many have left their original religious path searching for inner peace. I was raised a good-Catholic-boy, and it was a constant struggle to do the right thing! Because, as a child, we are always focused on doing the externals properly. When to genuflect. When to make the sign of the cross. Memorizing prayers. And things like that. The Buddha said something helpful, *"Peace comes from within. Do not seek it without."*

I think everybody longs for peace. But, after years of searching, I know that inner peace cannot be a goal that we struggle to reach. Peace is the absence of war, the cessation of hostilities, the end of striving. If we stop the fighting, we will find peace.

Peace is not something to achieve. We cannot battle our way to it. It is something we are. Something we discover in stillness.

April 18
Where Love Begins

Leo Tolstoy (1828–1910) once said, *"I understand only because I love."* But how do we teach that to a child?

Native Americans had a wonderful idea with the cradle boards that enabled a mother to carry her baby back-to-back. Even the youngest child felt the warmth of her mother while looking out at the world and became comfortable with it. It is in such settings that a child develops joyful relationships with birds and flowers, breezes, clouds, and people.

This is the beginning of feeling at home in the universe — which is perhaps the beginning of love.

April 19
On A Hillside

Many years ago I sat on a hillside in Israel. It overlooked the Sea of Galilee. Behind me, on top of the little hill, was a fine stone church dedicated to Jesus' Sermon on the Mount. The part of the "Sermon" that stuck with me that day was, *"Blessed are the gentle, for the earth will be their heritage."*

There has been a lot of bloodshed in that land since I was there but that moment of peace still resides in me.

Now, in my 80s, I sit on another hillside where I live. I look out and see the land and the people I love. Up the hill is our simple wooden chapel. And, the same beatitude is in my mind and heart — Blessed are the gentle, or meek, or humble, or simple.

We may get there in different ways, but I think everyone has a sacred hillside where the Sermon on the Mount is still being preached, encouraging each of us to be gentle, meek, humble, simple.

April 20
The Toad As Teacher

Meditation is now a common spiritual practice. But many people see it as a complex, specialized, and mysterious process. I wonder if we do not make too much of how to do it? Meditation can be a good thing, and can it not be a simple thing?

Lao Tzu (604–531 BCE?) is reported to have said, *"The way to do it is to be."* But how does one do that?

When frustrated about the "quality" of my meditation I like to consider the toad. We have one who seems to meditate all the time. This toad is not trying to achieve any high state. He is just being himself — like Lao Tzu recommends!

I find it helpful to take some time to imitate the toad. Just sitting and being myself. After all, isn't that what meditation really is? Or at least one way. Taking some time to quiet all the other voices, and just be myself.

Want to try it? Go ahead.

April 21
Me And Others Who
Are Vulnerable

I have not visited a jail much since I stopped practicing law half a century ago. But there is no shortage of folks I find imprisoned by old age, sickness, poverty, or in some way marginalized by a high-speed society. I can't solve most of their problems, but I can acknowledge that we belong to the same family.

The call for compassion is found throughout the Bible and in most sacred texts. In Matthew's Gospel, Jesus said *"In so far as you did this to one of the most vulnerable you have done it to me."* If we want to encounter the divine element in our lives, we only have to develop an empathetic response to our sisters and brothers. Which is a way of recognizing we are all dependent on each other.

APRIL 22
CLIMBING A LADDER

Once looking out on a beautiful late-April landscape, it seemed as if everything was growing. I could see the stages of plant and animal life. It is a seamless process. But what about us?

I've often found human growth to be like a ladder. We climb up to a rung. Then we regain our composure. In time we become comfortable on the rung. Perhaps we even become an expert concerning this rung. We do not want to become a struggling beginner again.

Yet if we remember that each step is only a rung, then we will welcome the freshness of each beginning. Then every step we take in life, even our final day, becomes an act of renewal.

The practical medieval mystic Meister Eckhart (1260–1328) left us this guidance about spiritual growth, *"You must always be a beginner among beginners."*

APRIL 23
FIND YOUR OWN LIGHT

I can't look around at all the new life springing forth without wondering how it all started, although I know the answer will never present itself to me. So I fantasize. Was there, as some suggest, another evolution before the physical one? A spiritual big bang before the physical one? I know we are all composed of stardust. Was that the beginning or the middle of the story? Pretty big stuff.

Reducing everything to a personal level, it began when I was very young. I was told that gods existed who were more powerful than adults, and I believed. But when I grew tall enough to look directly at the face of a god, I discovered it was only a mask, and I got angry. So I turned away from the god-mask. As The Buddha is reported to have said, *"Doubt everything. Find your own light."*

My childhood experience could have been the end of my relationship with the concept of God, because it filled me with doubt. But I've found that even doubt can be holy. It can guide us on much deeper paths to refreshing sacred realities.

April 24
The Church Door
And The Rain

Way-way-back when traditional religious institutions were still a part of my life, the church door was a symbol of the contrasts in life. As an adolescent I took comfort in the ritual of stepping from the world of emotional uncertainty, family illness, the restrictions of not much money, and

all the things everyone I knew struggled with — through the door — into the cool and quiet of the empty church — feeling the holy water on my hand and head — genuflecting to an unseen creative presence. Do I miss that? Yes, but I have found that the church door is not essential to the process.

Now, I stand to meet the rain, not kneel. And I feel the water from nowhere on my head and my hands. Yes, I can taste it. And I somehow know that I am where I ought to be.

APRIL 25
A GREY WORLD

A friend was in a conversation with an acclaimed Middle-European film maker who said contrast was the essence of his art. Contrast — in human history and in our individual lives. To the extent that I understand this, he means that if a person in Middle-Europe was born before the Soviet Union collapsed in 1991–92 he/she would have been in a culture where, as one imprisoned Russian poet put it, "Grey Is The Color Of Hope." And, grey is made up of a mixture of both white and black. In that mixture can be found the deep and fundamental meaning of a person's existence. So contrast and art go together.

I look at pictures of children crying in war-torn areas. And then elsewhere, protected and privileged youth concerned about what pleasures to choose on a spring day. Is recognizing the sacred in all life a means of finding one world to live in? Finding contrast on all our paths? Are there answers? Probably, but I have yet to find them — but I am working on it.

April 26
It Can't Hurt

About 40 years ago, here where I live, we had many beautiful Monarch butterflies at this time of year. For a long time, there have been none. Primarily this has to do with the destruction of a needed ecology thousands of miles away. Two years ago a couple of folks here, in my opinion, fell for an ad for "Butterfly Garden" seeds. Seemed silly but I ordered them. The seeds produced a colossal mess of ugly plants and attracted no butterflies!

Last year, to my surprise the plants appeared again and bloomed. This year they came back. And, yesterday I saw the first Monarch in years gracefully fly by! Was it because of the seeds? Well, it is just like prayer and meditation — it can't hurt!

What do I take away from all this? When good people do good things, in time, something good happens. So plant those seeds. We may never see what blooms, but it is the right thing to do.

April 27
Nothing Special

Life's greatest riches are often wrapped in plain paper, and when we open the box it is empty. There is a story about two students who enter the same spiritual center.

The first one only sees classes to attend, rules to discover, some dishes to wash, some time to be quiet. He is patient. He waits. Everything is ordinary. Finally, he is bored and leaves. The environment is not at all like his fantasy of a contemplative life.

The second student does not look outside, but listens inside. Her own inner voice translates for her the songs of the house. For her this is the beginning of the most exciting adventure that life can offer. She sees many magnificent happenings around her. She understands that all these wonderful things are just an ordinary part of life.

I've often found that if I am looking for something special, I probably just passed it.

April 28
New Paths

There are old, official paths across the meadow of our spiritual heritages, and they are still recommended by some. Those old paths are worn out and not very inviting to most people.

But the meadow itself is fresh and vibrant, always growing and changing. It would be a tragic mistake to abandon the meadow when we reject the old paths. There can be many new refreshing paths into this magnificent landscape.

Ralph Waldo Emerson (1803–1882) once wrote, *"Do not go where the path may lead, go instead where there is no path and leave a trail."*

Today we are all needed to find those new paths through the sacred landscape of life.

April 29
A Tree Grows and
So do We

I have come to believe that in order to live, we must grow. But how do we do that?

Growth can only be natural, as the ancient tree puts forth fresh leaves each year and it bears fruit on wood that is new and supple. All that we require for growth is contained within us at birth, so it is by looking inward that we find the wisdom to grow.

No matter how old we become, there is within us a child with our name. That young person has the same freshness at ninety-nine as at nine. But maybe not the same energy!

The point is —when it comes to life and growth, all we need is to simply be who we are.

April 30
The Arrow

All our lives our heart has been singing a little soundless song. Taking the time to listen to this song in each of our hearts is vital to every spiritual tradition because each of our individual hearts is also tuned to a great silent song of existence itself. It goes by many names. The names don't matter. I'm comfortable with "The Spirit."

If we open the door of our hearts, the wind of the Spirit will come like an arrow to a target. All we have to do is to find a space within us where we might uncover that target and wait for what we cannot hear or see.

The arrow knows what to do. That is all that is necessary.

MAY

MAY 1
A ROSE AMONG THORNS

In Hawaii "May Day" is "Lei Day." A big component of the festival is making colorful flower leis for friends. I learned a lei is a powerful gift.

One day I was visiting Kalaupapa, the former leper colony on Molokai, and was troubled by the suffering and agony of those who had lived there. In the late afternoon I returned to the neighboring island of Maui where I was staying with my family. We attended a luau organized by local children. I went, but my mind was still at Kalaupapa. This somber preoccupation was interrupted by a young dancer, about 10, who had apparently left the nearby stage in response to my sad expression. He was suddenly standing beside me. Slowly the boy took the lei from his neck and placed it on mine — with a kiss on my forehead — and a laugh. Damien, the famous "leper-priest" whose grave I had visited earlier that day, once said, *"Our Lord permits us now and then to pick a beautiful rose among sharp thorns."* The dancer had returned to the stage. He was smiling and so was I.

I kept that lei for years, until the last petal turned to dust.

MAY 2
A SIMPLE VIOLET

A reminder — the poet Basho (1644–1694) wrote "*On the mountain path, what is this special thing? A simple violet.*" I often feel that I am living amongst violet seekers. We may start out with dreams of glory, on high mountain passes, but somewhere along the line we realize that the simple violet is what deeply satisfies us.

This month fields are filled with small flowers of many colors. Being of an age when I have to watch where I put my feet, I become very aware of these annual carpets of tiny flowers. They aren't with us long. You don't want to blink!

This is the day of the
little purple flowers —
Hello and Goodbye!

If we are looking to find a spiritual compass in nature, May is a very special month. All we have to do is to look down at our feet. Is that a little yellow flower? Is that a freshly-born ladybug crawling up the stem? Can these things guide us toward feeling a bit more at home in the universe? A bit less anxious about life's challenges? Fellow violet–seekers, let us look today for something small and "unimportant" that we will remember for a long time!

MAY 3
GRAFTING

Flying around the world, in hopes that I might in some small way improve it, has been a major part of my life for so many years I cannot remember when it started. But I know that part is ending.

My father was born in 1899, and he never flew anywhere. But he often sat on a bench he had made, slowly drank his coffee, and gazed at an apple tree where he had grafted five different apple varieties at different times in his life. There is much more to our lives than "the beginning", "the middle", "the end." Our life-experience has to do with understanding how we graft with all parts of existence. In this way we make ever-widening circles.

Despite my differences with every other person, there are nonetheless times when I walk on common ground with everyone else. One of them will be trying my best to complete a final life- circle, and in that process it may be more helpful to reflect on an old apple tree than to plan a final world excursion.

MAY 4
CONTRADICTIONS

I say to my friend, "I look out my window and see a robin on the bare limb of the tree." Like an ancient haiku master he quickly responds, "So what season is it?" And I am transported to a well- known section of the Hebrew Bible — *"For everything there is a season."* (Qoheleth/ Ecclesiates 3: 1–8)

In nature, this is truly a season of contradictions. A daffodil opens up in the morning only to be assaulted by a heavy frost at night. As a Taoist writer put it; *"On misery perches happiness. Beneath happiness crouches misery."* They are connected.

A mountain must have two sides. Where I live, the north slope is quiet and passive. The forest grows unattended. We walk alone in the stillness. The south side is sunny and active. Here we farm and harvest. This is like the irritating parables of Jesus in which we find a personal challenge but one that cannot be explained by the rational mind alone, such as:

We played the pipes for you, and you wouldn't dance. We sang dirges, and you wouldn't cry. (Luke 7:31–35)

Dancing and crying. Laughter and tears. Birth and death. Robin and bare branch. They all have a place in this unique and wonderful journey we are each making through life. How does it work?

It just does.

May 5
Simple Gifts

The time between the first blossoms on the fruit trees and the beginning of planting in the garden is a unique window of opportunity, both in nature and in the personal psyche of anyone touched by the Judeo-Christian-Islamic heritage. It is a time to examine the balance in our lives; even in strictly secular circles, this time of year presents an occasion for reflection on the way we live.

Ours has become a culture of increased technology and acquisition. Could it be at some deep level we all understand that we have lost something in that process? This is a concern even in the area of spiritual growth. Perhaps this awareness has something to do with our cultural roots going back to simpler times — the wilderness, the desert, Walden Pond.

Chapter 48 of *THE TAO*, The Way, points out:

> *In the pursuit of learning, every day something is added. In the pursuit of the Tao every day something is dropped.*

Can we drop something today?

MAY 6
IN OUR PRAYERS

When we wish to help provide an environment of sacred strength around those who can't do that for themselves at the moment, the first essential step is to forget about our own personal troubles and agendas. In fact, to forget ourselves for a while. We then stand in that incredible landscape representing those who have asked for our support, and for all those in the world who are more oppressed than ourselves. When we empty out our own preoccupations, space is provided for empathy and compassion. Standing there quietly, just by being there, we are truly praying on behalf of those we love and of those we have never met. It may not make sense, but it does seem to be beneficial.

When Quakers think of someone facing challenges they sometimes call it "Holding in the light." It is recognition of the sacred spark within each of us. It is also an acknowledgment that, in some way, the common joys and sorrows of life unite and strengthen us all. People need not find themselves alone when times are tough.

So if, directly or implicitly, someone asks for you to stand with them spiritually, you may be asking yourself, "How do I do that?" Don't worry about it. There is an old monastic adage, *"Trying to pray is praying."*

MAY 7
SILVER BELL

Near the end of his life the Japanese poet and lay-priest Issa (1763–1828) was walking in the early morning to a Buddhist temple. He sat down to rest and his eyes fell on some flowers along the path. Then the great Temple Bell began to ring as the monks solemnly opened the morning prayer service. A simple but profound poem jumped into Issa's mind which I think roughly translates something like this,

Listening to the Temple Bell or
watching the flowers open — it's all the same!

If we, like Issa, pause to take those moments of rest in life, or better yet, search them out, we may hear our destiny tinkling like a distant silver bell.

If the bell sounds like a temple bell and I yearn for spiritual solitude, I might realize that I am already in my own monastery. Our contemplative journeys may well unfold in the bustle of a noisy city.

May 8
When the Soul Sighs

Many of us find something holy and helpful in doubt, and understand what the German author Jean Paul (1763–1825) meant when he wrote, "God is an unutterable sigh, planted in the depths of the soul."

"God" is a word, but not the final word. It is not the treasure at the end of the quest. "God" is not the answer to all our questions, but the ultimate question. We are finite beings groping for the infinite. No one of us will ever encounter the whole concept. Yet each of us will touch a part of ultimate reality. In the groping we will sometimes comprehend a divine element which will be "up there," "out there," "in here" or all over the place. When we are seriously ill it is often easier to reach out to a being existing in a better place than where we find ourselves. At the same time, there can be moments when we know there is no distance between ourselves and "God".

For most of our pilgrimage, it is enough to know that "God?" is a question through which we experience something of the mystery of reality. The soul's sigh can be understood best on the quiet north side of the mountain. It is a still, yin experience; a whisper moving gently through the right side of the brain, tickling and awakening something we knew before we were born.

"God" is fundamentally a question about what it means to be human. It is only within the human adventure that our relation to the Divine gets its meaning.

MAY 9
STILL BEARING FRUIT

We can learn about aging from old apple trees and Zen teachers. When our small community first moved to an abandoned farm there were ancient apple trees, some planted in the 19th century. Often there was not much left of the tree, a hollow trunk and one or two branches. Sometimes, in what would be the tree's final year, it would have one very large apple, and nothing else. I saw it as fruit, but the tree was producing seed.

When it became clear that a wonderful Zen Roshi in the Bay Area was dying, his many students were very sad. As the story was told to me, one day he got out of his sick-bed and announced, "It is time to make noodles." He crowded all the students into the kitchen and they began making noodles. At noon they kept going. At sunset they were still at it. One person told me noodles "were coming out of the window" — probably an exaggeration. Finally, the Roshi stopped. Everyone was smiling. This day of working together was the impression he wanted to leave with them.

It is sometimes difficult for loving family and caregivers to understand that which might appear to be dangerously eccentric is a senior planting seeds that he/she will never see mature. Have patience. We old ones are just "doing our thing."

Our dreams must always lead us toward the opening of new buds. It is part of flowing with the river of life.

MAY 10
WHERE FLOWERS GROW

I only recently became aware that decay is part of the beauty in life. Going back to the roses that burst out this month — it is wonderful to move between the bushes and collect blooms of different shades to combine into a bouquet which sits like an art treasure on the dining room table. I always regretted it when the petals dropped. Dead flowers! Get fresh ones! But recently I read a poet's suggestion that the full cycle of the rose, including the decline of its "perfect beauty," was something to be experienced. I started arranging fallen petals around the bottom of the vase. Every rose I watched travel from my sense of its perfection into total collapse has taken a singular path.

Thanks to a poet, whose identity I cannot recall, I have learned to appreciate the rose itself, not my image of it. It is not enough for me to have strolled through eighty-five months of May as if I were a visitor to a flower exhibition.

Delightful sights. Pleasant breezes. Lovely smells. Charming birds and butterflies. I must learn to accept all the seasons of life, including decline.

MAY 11
IT IS NOT ALL ABOUT ME

Seeing God in others is sometimes difficult for me. I frequently look on people as a hindrance to inner peace. Yet it is in the human community that I have most often discovered not only the presence of the sacred but a deeper understanding of my own humanity.

One of the things I have learned is that if I attempt to stand alone in my spiritual growth, I will feel lonely and uncomfortable. Jewish history emphasized the community rather than focusing on each individual person. A particular individual might be off the track, but when the community, the people, were going along alright, that benefited every person in the community.

Accepting that each individual is connected to the spiritual well-being of the community means that everyone has some responsibility to help the community be healthy.

MAY 12
A GENTLE BREEZE

I am fond of the story in 1 Kings (19:11–13) where Elijah is trying to encounter Yahweh. First came a mighty wind — no Yahweh. Then came an earthquake — no Yahweh. Then came a fire — no Yahweh. *"Then came the sound of a gentle breeze"* and there Elijah found Yahweh. Something similar has been experienced in other cultures.

As winter comes to an end in the Western United States, Native Americans in many places are mindful of a wind that causes the snow pack to lessen or disappear in a few hours. In the Pacific Northwest and parts of Northern California it is known as the "Chinook Wind."

I first experienced it on the banks of the Columbia River where the Chinook culture once thrived. A light, warm wind comes up the river from the Pacific coast. With it comes the smell of the sea, and the earth, and growing things. The bite of winter disappears. It might return but anyone who smelled the Chinook knew winter's time was limited. I was a tie-wearing, briefcase-carrying, intense, twenty-something lawyer. But I somehow knew that I was standing where some Chinook man or woman once stood centuries ago. The world that preoccupied each of us had retreated before this sweet breeze. There is some variation of that Columbia riverbank to be found near every stream, hillside, and backyard in North America. The promises of existence are in those gentle breezes.

MAY 13
GO TO THE PINE

When my children were quite young, we started writing haiku poems together. One day my young son was struggling with the use of a pine tree in a haiku. I remembered the advice of the poet Basho (1644–1694) *"If you want to know about the pine, go to the pine tree!"* And that is what we did.

My son's ideas about "pine" changed as he pulled back the pine branches and stuck his face near the trunk of a specific tree. This was the beginning of our "haiku walks." We quietly strolled outside looking for little moments that could be the basis of a poem. It was rare that either of us actually wrote a poem. The walks became valuable experiences in themselves, as if we were reading the poem in nature.

It is exciting to go over familiar ground and find something unexpected. My children and I have seen, really seen, frosty spider webs reflecting the sunlight, the first squash blossom unfolding, plum petals dropping on an amazed cat, bees on the rosemary, tall trees going in and out of view in the mist, a little bird on a frozen woodpile, orange butterflies circling the chapel, and many, many ordinary things in an extraordinary way. We would come back from any haiku walk loaded with tales, and the occasional poem, to share with others. We also came back refreshed and more confident about living on this planet.

MAY 14
BELIEF OR SUPERSTITION?

No one can believe in everybody's God. Jews, Christians, and Muslims have to stretch to take in Native American creation stories. Buddhists have trouble with Christian concepts of a personal god. I do not want to believe in the God presented by fundamentalists of any religious persuasion, and they would not be satisfied with my understanding of God. We are all both believers and nonbelievers. And that is good.

The Spanish writer and social activist José Bergamin (1895–1983) who spent a lifetime, often in exile, trying to find a breathing space between various religious and political absolutists wrote: *"A belief which leaves no place for doubt is not a belief; it is a superstition."*

"God" is a word for something absolute that is beyond our ability to express, conceptualize, or objectify. Whenever someone tries to ignore that mystery and presents the divine in a simplistic manner, doubt is not only understandable, it is necessary.

MAY 15
DIFFERENT WINDOWS

The circumstances of our individual pilgrimages are unique, and no two people experience "God", whatever that may mean to us, in the same way. We each live in a room fashioned by our life stories. Our rooms differ.

Even the shapes of our windows to the world are different. When the morning light comes and dispels the darkness, it enters each of our lives according to the shape of our individual windows. Life experience may make some windows large and others small, some are narrow, some round and some square or in exotic shapes.

Yet we share the same light. When we rise and encounter the warmth and vitality of this light, we are all opening ourselves to the ultimate frontier of existence.

MAY 16
JUDGE NOT

I have come to the belief that we judge others because we judge ourselves. Since we judge ourselves, we assume others are also judging us. So we point to another person in order to divert attention away from the faults that we find in our own lives.

I find this to be a dangerous game. When judging another person's conduct we attempt to exile

the accused from the human family, and none of us has a right to do that. Perhaps if we stop judging ourselves we will refrain from judging others.

The past will take care of itself—jump into the present. If we try to float on yesterday's wave, then we'll miss the wave that is beneath us now — the wave that is ready to carry us away on the voyage of life.

MAY 17
THE DUCK

In 1910 when my mother was in the first grade, she was given a bowl and told to paint a duck at the bottom of it. The teacher laughed at the results and Mom never drew anything more for the rest of her life! That was very sad, for everyone is an artist.

The artist in us lives at our center. If our preoccupations can be distracted, then our bodies can become the medium for expressing a message from our inner-self in a concrete form that can be seen with our eyes and felt with our hands. This is often an expression of the truest part of ourselves. A glimpse at what is most natural and genuine.

And, never laugh at anyone's art!

MAY 18
DOING THE RIGHT THING

One morning, I was standing in our fields looking at the tiny new olive buds and finding a bird's nest with newborns peering over the edge. The next day, I was in Boston watching graduates from several institutions in gowns rushing up and down Huntington Avenue. It is a time of new beginnings. It is also a time of uncertainty.

As we respond to the uncertainties we all face at this moment in our personal story and in history, will we foster divisions and search for a safe niche, or will we have faith in the common ground on which we all walk?

It seems to me this is something young people are grasping. Sure, there are still many who are only looking after themselves. But a growing number are working for change in the world in politics, communities, non-profits, spiritual groups. I love the name of one rather fundamentalist college social action program — "Get dirty for Jesus."

Social justice goes back far beyond Jesus. *Tikkun olam*, "repairing the world", is an ancient Jewish reminder of the need to care for one another. Why? Because it is right.

MAY 19
SECRET GOOD DEEDS

In many Zen monasteries there exists a practice known as *Injigyo*. It is often translated as "secret good deeds." The members of the monastic family do surprising little things to help each other sense that they are living in a community of concern. At night a tear in a robe is mended. Bathrooms are cleaned. Clothes are hung out to dry and also rescued from a sudden downpour. Favorite foods show up at odd times and places.

The underpinning of these practices begins with learning to look outside ourselves and our concerns to see what is happening to others nearby. An elderly neighbor who has trouble walking finds his morning paper next to his door and not in the driveway. A frantic and hassled teenager wakes up to find her papers and notes all collected and nicely organized in her backpack. You all know what I'm talking about.

As I started moving into old-age, I often thought that it was enough if I took care of my own needs and did not burden someone else. But I need to look outside myself more. There is always time and energy to do something for someone nearby so that he or she knows they live in an environment where compassion matters. And from that, I truly believe, comes the only hope we have for a world of kindness and peace.

Today I want to find more opportunities for "secret good deeds." Will you join me?

May 20
Breath of Life

Around this time of year, Christians celebrate the Feast of Pentecost, which commemorates a day the followers of Jesus, *"had all met in one room, when suddenly they heard what sounded like a powerful wind from heaven, the noise of which filled the entire house in which they were sitting; and something appeared to them that seemed like tongues of fire; these separated and came to rest on the head of each of them. They were filled with the Holy Spirit, and began to speak foreign languages..."* [Acts 2:1–4] For me this is a time for finding the common ground in many faith traditions. Related to Shavuot, the Jewish harvest festival, Pentecost commemorates the coming of the Spirit, the promised Comforter, into the void of fear and confusion left by the execution of Jesus.

I have long focused on that *powerful wind from heaven*. All during my young Catholic life the hymn *Veni Sancti Spiritus* (Come Holy Spirit) was a truly powerful mantra. As I grew older, the Chinese concept of *ch'i* (or *qi* as it is now spelled in English) fascinated me. The character consists of lines representing breath, as on a cold day, combined with a symbol of universal nourishment. *Ch'i* is sometimes translated as "life force" or "spiritual energy." Most people on

the planet have probably sensed some nourishing breath
of life. We may have trouble defining it but we seem to
recognize it.

MAY 21
LIGHT ONE CANDLE

When Peter Benenson (1921–2005) founded Amnesty International he said, "*It is better to light a candle than to curse the darkness.*" That is a healthy attitude.

I have little hope for a major cultural revolution. In the 1960s, I felt that we could change the world with broad strokes! Then on a nearby campus four students protesting a war were shot and killed — May 4, 1970. After that I no longer sensed that the *Age of Aquarius* was dawning.

When we light any candle, its tiny flame must be protected. It can be blown out by ideology, whether that comes from obstructionists on the right or politically correct true-believers on the left — or from the rigidity of our twisted religious history.

However, as I stand looking out on the porch of our little chapel in the spring twilight, I can sense people beyond number carrying their little candles and protecting the flames from the storms around us. In those fragile lights is the beauty of our age and the hope of our future.

MAY 22
A LEAF GOSPEL

Who was Jesus? Once the Protestant reformer Martin Luther (1483–1546) suggested we look *"not in books alone but in every leaf in springtime."* That is good advice.

When I do look in a book it is often Luke's gospel, which was probably written about A.D. 85–90. I don't think Luke was waiting for a second coming. He encouraged his readers to encounter the divine in daily life.

Luke's image of Jesus portrays a humanistic savior interested in the poor, the oppressed, and the

outcasts. And, in ordinary life — *"in every leaf in springtime"*.

May 23
Surrounded By Wonders

At this time of year, it is easy to find and to celebrate the sacred in every growing person and thing around us. Emily Dickinson (1830–1886) wrote, "*To live is so startling it leaves little time for anything else.*"

The greatest danger is when delight turns to drudgery as we limit our awareness to a list of things to be done. The garden must be watered, weeded, harvested. There is no time to contemplate roses as we spray them for blackspot. And the first squash blossom may go completely unnoticed as we are fighting with the aphids.

The most important thing to be done is to open ourselves to the marvels of the season!

May 24
Where I Belong

There are times problems overload my emotional system. Everyone knows that anguish. News we did not want to hear from a doctor. Family members or friends taking a wrong turn. The promise of college evaporating. Money in short supply. Not being able to help when you want to. For the aged, and I am one of them, watching institutions we contributed to and relied upon crumbling. Lack of energy. Lack of memory. And on and on and on.

If I am prudent, that is a time to step outside and walk among the ancient trees. The wind plays in their tops, but their trunks stand firm. And at their base a family of quail cautiously sets out to forage through the grass. There is also a history in this grass. Here are grains planted by pioneers or dropped by birds a century ago, now ripening with fascinating heads. I suspect some ancient species are also here, which managed to escape time and have a cycle of existence that is yet to be discovered.

I am surrounded by a story bigger than my own. This is a place where I belong.

May 25
Young Prophets

There are a lot of spiritually-questioning young adults. Some call them "nones" because they say check "none of the above" when presented with a list of religious denominations. It used to be simple. Parents went to church and adolescents rejected the whole scene.

I don't want young people to throw out everything because they have serious problems with clergy or creed or institutions. There is a whole spiritual heritage they are heir to and entitled to use as enrichment in their lives. I also want them to understand that personal doubt is really holy and natural. A religious organization which does not accept this is twisted and probably soul- dead. All questioning is holy for all of us.

Our spiritual life must be reformed and refreshed, and this is partly possible by questioning and reformulating our understanding of the sacred dimensions of life. And, we must trust our experiences. That is a bad word in some hierarchies, for experience is beyond the control of authority, and I will admit it can be a two-edged sword. A young child opens her heart to a fundamentalist view of

God. Then she is burned by the realities of church life and her journey of becoming a person. She may be too hurt to ever open up again. There are secret tears in many of the young cynics I have met.

Our actual experiences, positive and negative, are the only lasting foundations we have for faith, hope and love.

MAY 26
SANDALS

We need to accept many aspects of life rather than to attempt to control or eliminate them, as is the American tendency. It is a simple but important lesson, for example, to train a child that when the house is chilly you put on a sweater rather than running to turn up the thermostat. This has a direct relationship to the spiritual life. On the one hand, there is an awareness of a situation and a personal response to it. The alternative is simply to find a solution which eliminates the problem. The quest for a push-button spirituality is often a problem during adolescence and young adulthood.

This fundamental difference of approach has been described in many religious traditions. There is a Buddhist tale which concerns two monks walking along a very rough road. They have been on it for a long time. One monk says, "If they covered this road with leather, it would certainly make traveling much easier." The other monk responds, "I think if I covered my feet with leather, it would be enough."

The first talks about what "they" ought to do and the other takes personal responsibility. The first, in effect, does not wish to be aware of anything outside of his own comfort. The other is beginning to harmonize with life.

May 27
New Life, Ordinary Clothes

I ssa (1763–1828) wrote:

> We started the spring in our ordinary clothes... me and the
> sparrow.

But what is spiritually uplifting about birds?

There in the meadow, or the park, or the space in the sidewalk cracks, the sparrow with her customary drab plum-
age finds new life where nothing had been living.

Look, when you are in your mid-80's as I am, you blink and
the world you knew is gone. It can get rather depressing.
Then you blink again and there is new life where there
had been none, and your faith in the human adventure is
restored.

Follow the simple sparrow in her ordinary clothes.

MAY 28
A SENSE OF RENEWAL
ON A SPRING NIGHT

R ecently I was bothered by some sad news and I couldn't sleep. I decided to move from my worried little world outside into what I am comfortable calling "God's Big World."

On such a night there is a sense of life going on forever. Every place around me was a mystery, not asking to be explained but simply experienced. And there are all those little things— sweet smells, gentle breezes, the blinking lights of a jet plane, and the stars. For a while, I remained still and tried to be open to that sense of renewal, for me, for those I love, and for our world.

I read somewhere that everything on our planet, including each of us, was formed from stardust. Maybe that is why this vast universe in the night sky does not feel alien. The waning moon spreads a soft rosy light. This moon is called "The Strawberry Moon" by my Pomo neighbors. It signals the time for the Strawberry Festival which celebrates the renewal of life.

216

I started back to the house with a feeling similar to when I listen to a great piece of music. It ends, but still somehow remains with me as I walk out of the concert hall and onto the street.

Entering my room, without turning the light on, I walked past the cat, still asleep on "his" chair. I guess it's natural for him to rest in God's world all through the night. That night I did as well.

May 29
New Leaves

As with every living thing, each of us is either growing or decaying. There is no middle ground.

The ancient tree puts forth fresh leaves each year and it bears fruit on wood that is new and supple. There is within the tree the same vitality which produced fruit in its first season. No matter how old we become there is within each of us a child waiting to be born. That youthful person has the same freshness at ninety-nine as at nine.

In order to live, we must grow. How? By gently unfolding our potential through practicing the art of living. Each day we must stretch a little into the uncomfortable. But we ought not to seek perfection. Denounce perfection. Growth is natural. Only when we attempt to arrest the process and remain immature will decay begin. And, with decay comes a decline in our vital energy.

There is always within each of us a hunger for life. Let the fresh leaves come forth.

MAY 30
FIRST BREATH,
LAST BREATH

Dying is not simply an absence of life. It is a part of living. Certain creatures know little about dying and almost nothing about death. Some insects lay their eggs in October and then die. The eggs hatch in June. Half of the year is completely unknown to these small creatures, but it does not matter. They live their lives completely. Can I also live a full existence, without knowing what lies beyond my last breath?

A Zen master once summed up all wisdom on the art of living by commanding:

When you eat – eat. / When you sleep – sleep.

We could add another couplet:

When you live—live. / When you die—die.

Death is not the enemy. Francis of Assisi (1182–1226) called it "Our Sister."

MAY 31
A TIME TO REMEMBER

Near the end of May, we in the United States observe Memorial Day to remember those who died in wars. Most people forget about the reason for the holiday and simply see it as the beginning of the summer season. That is regrettable.

The price of war was recently brought home to me as I stood in a Bay Area National Cemetery where so many of the youth and the dreams of our nation are buried. At my feet were the remains of those who had experienced the horrors of war. Behind me was the beauty and peace of San Francisco Bay.

I tried to open my heart to imagine a voice from the graves of a few I knew. It was something

like, "Hey, nice day for a picnic!" Not very profound. Or, maybe it was. Remembering those who die in wars might be a way of decreasing our wars.

JUNE

June 1
Fresh Starts

This month is a time of educational endings and beginnings. High School graduations mark the completion of increasingly demanding school experiences. Then college begins — the next race for students and parents.

Leo Tolstoy (1828–1910) wrote, *"June is the time of plans and projects."* It is truly a wonderful time for fresh starts and a popular month for new commitments and adventures.

But it is also a rewarding time for just sitting and being aware of what is happing around us and within us. In nature there is no race, it should be the same in our spiritual growth. In both cases what is celebrated is the unfolding itself.

JUNE 2
SQUASH BLOSSOMS

Silently it comes in the early light of dawn—the first squash blossom!

Many years ago I learned from a Hopi friend that the beautiful trumpet of a squash announces the nourishment and survival of a people. I really fell into that outlook on life. For me it starts in June with the sudden blossoming of the humble zucchini squash. And it goes on all through summer and well into the autumn with the majestic pumpkin. Even when there is a touch of frost, the last beautiful blossom may appear.

Someplace back in my heritage there must've been a squash or pumpkin clan, because I really resonate with these vegetable cousins. And the human ones also. In a burst of romanticism while standing on a hillside looking down at a Hopi village before coming to the famous mesas, I felt at home. Then I was told that place had been settled by the Squash Clan many centuries ago. Boy that did it!

I was told that squash and pumpkin helped shift a number of Native American cultures from hunters to farmers. The Hopi felt this was in the direction of a healthier and more peaceful society, with a concern for the common good. Maybe the squash blossoms are still pointing that way!

June 3
The Wind And The Walls

I'm very conscious of winds this time of year. They move through the branches of trees in marvelous ways, playing them like musical instruments. I also think there is a wind of something we might call the Life-Spirit which moves through and plays each of us in ways which are helpful to one another.

However, building walls around ourselves will only keep the wind of the Spirit from moving through us. Our strings will remain limp.

But if there is within us a nostalgia for freedom, we will chip at the walls we have built. Then one day the walls will dissolve like clay in the rain.

After that we, and others, will once again hear the music of our song.

JUNE 4
AN INNER LIGHT

No matter what thoughts come our way, or what feelings we experience, we always have a choice. It is a gift that we have all been given.

There is permanently implanted within each of us a light that longs for its nature and yearns to shine. We can always choose to let this light cut through the darkness.

Freedom and balance lies in learning how to use this choice — and in trusting what we discover.

When I was a small child, "God" was an explanation for things I did not understand. I only knew about humans, so God was a superhuman being who made things work. Since God was a being, he/she had to live somewhere. I vaguely understood that God was to be found "up there" I was not sure where "up there" was, but I was confident God did not live in the same place I did.

June 5
Looking For God's Address

As I matured, my concept of God slowly changed from superhuman to supernatural. God became

a spiritual supreme being who lived, not "up there," but everywhere at once. My supernatural God functioned in an incorporeal realm that was fundamentally different from my physical surroundings. God lived "out there"— outside of my world.

I started thinking about God again in my twenties while studying psychologists who focused attention on a divine element in human existence. The God of spiritual psychologists seemed to live not "up there" or "out there" but "in here." That was hard to put into words but it was some sort of experience which is the source of balance, joy, fulfillment, and meaning in life — perhaps even peace.

June 6
Mom's Afghan

When my mother was approaching seventy she began crocheting colorful squares. She wanted to give me something of her best craft before her eyesight failed. After several years, there were enough squares for her to put them together into an afghan.

She was blind when she died at eighty-five. During the winter months, this gift and memory is on my bed and much appreciated. It has also covered those I love in their last days.

Like my mother's afghan, a beneficial life is made up of little squares of spiritual experience which can be passed on as a precious heritage.

JUNE 7
ALL TOUCHED BY
ONE SPIRIT

It seems to me that there can no longer be an isolated spiritual life.

We are all mutual inhabitants of this earth at this particular moment in history—that is a significant point of common interest. To quest for God is to become involved in God's world, which involves each other.

I think the purpose of prayer, the keystone of spirituality, is not to escape from and deny life but rather to more fully comprehend it and live it. Perhaps recognizing each other along the way.

JUNE 8
JESUS OF NAZARETH AND
OTHERS NEGOTIATING THE
HUMAN EXPERIENCE

I am a lay monk with a Catholic heritage. But when approaching spiritual growth, I come at the subject as a Christian humanist. What often drives me through my meditations is the general exploration of what it means to become a person, to attempt to achieve our humanity as part of the reality of life, and to find the sacred within that process. I clumsily stumble along on a path made by countless people from Erasmus of Rotterdam (1466–1536) down through the centuries to our own day, and including a host of contemporary social reformers like Teilhard de Chardin (1881–1955), Dorothy Day (1897–1980), Dag Hammarskjöld (1905–1961), Dietrich Bonhoeffer (1906–1945), Thomas Merton (1915–1968), Oscar Romero (1917–1980), Sophie Scholl (1921-1943), Martin Luther King, Jr., (1929–1968), and many, many others walking the Way of Jesus of Nazareth while searching for a divine spark in the struggle for human worth, dignity, happiness, and meaning.

In this quest I am more comfortable with observable phe-
nomena than general theory. My values are existential
in that I am concerned with the individual choices to be
made in life and the need for authenticity and freedom.

In the rare moments when I can comprehend that it is part
of my essential nature to accept the grace to meet this challenge, I am no longer "monk," "parent," "spiritual coach,"
"humanist," or even "Christian." All facets converge in a
simple concern for living, which binds me to all my fellow
pilgrims with whom I share this moment of history.

JUNE 9
A TIME TO RETURN HOME

One warm afternoon in Assisi, during a very difficult time in my life, I visited Saint Francis's forest hermitage.

Eremo Delle Carceri, "the hermitage of the cells," is a random collection of small stone buildings.

There was obviously no master plan, but a remarkable beauty arises from the simple and authentic structures. The only sounds are the wings of birds, descendants of those to whom Francis (1182–1226) once preached.

I walked alone down a sylvan path and came upon an outdoor chapel. While standing before the plain stone altar, all the life questions that had been coming up in my mind faded away. A peace, perhaps a residue from Francis' time, came over me. I picked up a small stone near the altar.

In the healing stillness, I put the stone in my pocket and knew it was time to go home. Everyone comes across healing places at hard times — places which help us return to where we started. I still have the stone. In my soul that quiet place near Assisi will always be found.

JUNE 10
DIVINE CRAZINESS

My journey has long valued the spiritual. But spirituality and madness are parallel forces that are much more related to each other than is often acknowledged. A sojourn on either subjective path is a passport to the other. For many months and years of my life, I have crossed back and forth. It was especially so in the early days of AIDS pandemic when my days were focused on children who, like Morning Glory flowers, were blooming as best they could for the time they had.

It sometimes becomes necessary to surrender to the madness that we find in both life and death before we can find wholeness and peace.

There are many quiet moments in this life. As each of our stories unfolds there are also a number of startling situations. We live in the ordinary times and only survive the dramatic events.

In the final analysis, all we really have to share with each other is how we live. Madness is part of our spirituality — part of letting go.

June 11
The Grace to Dance

The way in which a person and a society live a wholesome and happy life is an ongoing quest. I think God left it largely to each generation to figure it all out for its own time.

It is reasonable to look to our religious traditions, but there is often a problem about how this wisdom is presented to us. If it is overly harsh and rigid, it is ineffective and counterproductive.

Rather than dogmas, we need to learn the steps in a dance of life that can be used in meeting difficult situations. Perhaps we can find these steps with each other, in nature, or in some utterly surprising place.

June 12
Anne and Nature

Anne Frank was born on this day in 1929. But she will forever be remembered as a teenager who died in a Nazi concentration camp when she was 15.

Anne had a frightening adolescence. But when she was 13 and only able to see a tree and a bit of the sky from an attic window, where her family was hiding she wrote, *The best remedy for those who are afraid, lonely, or unhappy is to go outside, somewhere where they can be quite alone with the heavens, nature, and God... I firmly believe that nature brings solace in all troubles.*

Quiet and solitude is part of the essence of our life here at Starcross. And we have recently shared that solace with others who were "afraid, lonely, or unhappy." Veterans from the vicious trauma of war. Those facing serious illness or loss. Courageous women who feel betrayed by institutions.

Young and old yearning to transcend the soul-sucking elements of life. There are no lectures here, only the space to hear the song of a bird. Looking at the wonderful things in a square foot of earth. Picking olives. Hoeing in the garden. Simply sitting still and being open to a night sky.

I trust what happens where I live is also somehow of help to those who will never visit but are part of the larger community of seekers whose connections we can sometimes feel. And, the sacred space which bonds a person with the simple beauty of nature does not have to be acres of rural land. It can be a flower pot on a window sill. Recently I was having some mobility problems on a trip to a foreign city. With my leg propped up, and feeling sorry for myself, I looked across the busy street and saw a woman bounce out of her flat onto a little balcony and water her herb pots. Instantly I felt that "all is as it should be."

Remembering Anne today, let each of us in our own way care for our flower pots as best we can and help bring a bit of sacred solace to whatever challenges we, or others, may face.

June 13
What Wonders

How do we become aware of the presence of the sacred in our lives? What are the tools with which we can refresh our faith as we move through the challenges of everyday life?

It was perhaps less difficult for our primitive ancestors who experienced the whole natural world as a sacred reality. The rational, the practical, the psychological, and the spiritual aspects of life were all integrated, and they were all sacred.

The quest for the sacred has continued to be a part of the way in which many, perhaps most, women and men have unfolded the wonder of their humanity. As Madeleine L'Engle (1918-2007) once wrote, *"There is nothing so secular that it cannot be sacred"*— she was right.

What will we allow to unfold today?

June 14
Inside This Moment

Frequently within our memory, there is something that may contain advice for the present and future. Corrie Ten Boom (1892–1983), a Dutch Christian watchmaker who hid many Jews from the Nazis and then worked for reconciliation after the war, wrote, *"Memories are the key not to the past, but to the future."*

Childhood memories have even been used by some psychological schools as part of the therapy process. Some Adlerian psychologists saw childhood recollections as a way to become aware of our present life style. They observed that a person's childhood recollections change as her or his life style alters. This doesn't work for everyone but occasionally I do try to recall my earliest childhood recollection. I often get a quick flash. Then I think of one or two more and try to find a common theme. Sometimes it results in a surprising and very simple point.

I do believe that the core of our unfolding story is inside each present moment. And memories can indeed be a key to the future.

June 15
The Waves

I live just a short drive away from the Pacific Ocean. I'm continually amazed by the ocean's beauty and power — its ability to renew itself with each passing tide.

I can't help reflecting that each of our lives, like the ocean, is made up of many waves. There are waves for each moment, each day, each year, each life.

When we find ourselves hungering for a sense of completeness, I've found it helpful to be in harmony with the waves. If we will just allow ourselves to jump into a now-moment, perhaps we might find the same renewal that the tides do.

JUNE 16
LOVE WATER AND RICE

An important contribution in Zen Buddhism is the thirteenth century document of the Soto school, *Instructions to the Chief Cook.* The kitchen master is told to find the essence of the spiritual life within *"a blade of grass."* Material for a great sermon comes from *"a particle of dust."* The cook must *"love water and rice as parents love children."*

It is the Western way to put down our great learning in complex thoughts wrapped in heavy books. Yet how we yearn, even hunger, for the simplicity of the Zen cook who finds theology not in the latest book but in a blade of grass or an obvious question.

JUNE 17
THE ROAD GOES ON

Most of the pain that I've experienced in my life has been pain related to loss. And that is an unavoidable part of life. Mine was a deeply sorrowful odyssey in which I lost children and friends to AIDS. There is nothing unique in my journey. It is inevitable that everyone encounters overpowering circumstances —all people will experience situations where the human spirit is in danger of destruction. Many, like myself, will be unaware of the peril until they have been hurt.

In those dark times of World War II, some survived the horrors of the Nazi concentration camps with a stronger spiritual faith and trust in life. Some did not.

No matter what hazard we encounter or how vulnerable we may be, for most of us the road goes on. And, hopefully we will rediscover ways that lead to deeper meaning and satisfaction in our lives.

JUNE 18
TOWARD INNER HARMONY

We each travel through different countries. In our journeys we have come upon a few idyllic sites and many frightening abysses. For every person there seems to be a different form of hell and heaven.

But one thing we all share with every woman and man in history is the often torturous struggle to keep moving toward a place of inner harmony.

There will always be many hardships. But there is also to be found many joyful paths of happiness and spiritual fulfillment.

June 19
Beyond The Tattered World

Living is a complex process. The ways we relate to each other sometimes seem increasingly superficial, and the problems we face progressively more profound. Have we made some fundamental miscalculations about what it means to be human?

I would love to retrace history's steps a bit, searching for some simplicity. This is not an attempt to find a protective niche from adversity. There is no personal exemption from the pains of my age. AIDS. Wars. Terrorism. Famine. Destruction of nature. Drugs. Violence. Homelessness. Anxiety. Fear. The empty sense of self. The lust for power. Dishonesty. Manipulation. Cynicism. Mistrust. These are the sick and unavoidable realities of my world. But there is more to existence.

For years I have concentrated too much on the cracks. Now I want to look through the broken window, to include in my experience not only the tattered world but also the stars.

I have an intense longing to comprehend the whole human experience. To do this perhaps I must also find the evolving Divinity dwelling in the life I share with my neighbors on this planet.

June 20
Toward The Center

The circle of my spiritual life is becoming clearer to me. Out on the edges, where there are dragons in Tibetan paintings, are people I have disappointed or hurt. Threatening people. But there also are all the self-destructive tendencies in my own inner life. There are to be found the indifferent churchmen of my time as well as all the bad spiritual choices I have made: pride over humility, security over openness, and hundreds of shallow diversions.

As I move from the turbulent outer limits toward the center of my life, I encounter solid sanctuaries of peace; nature, spiritual communities that nourish, my family, friends, memories, all surrounding an open space that is life and God. Each of these are dynamic and changing, and all require me to be alert and aware.

At the center of the sacred circle of my life, of anyone's life, is life itself. I am comfortable using the word "God" for this realm into which we all must, at some time, go.

June 21
Midsummer

One of June's great commemorations is the Summer Solstice. Shakespeare wrote *A Midsummer Night's Dream*, Mendelssohn composed music for it. Behind these great works are centuries of fiery nights and frenzied dances. The Druids, and probably others, felt the Summer Solstice was an important touching of heaven and earth.

My family's acknowledgement of the solstice is very mild, compared to Shakespeare, Mendelssohn, and the Druids. We have a special dessert and sit outside looking at the stars. We want to experience in some way this shortest night of the year.

Before entering the well-lit house, I am wondering what fairies, elves, and angels may be in the shadows. It is easy to imagine we hear Shakespeare's Oberon,

> *Now, until the break of day ... each fairy take his gate; and each several chamber bless, through this place with sweet peace; e'er shall it in safety rest ...*

Ah ...

June 22
Angelus

There is not as much resistance to morning meditation and prayer as there is to taking a spiritual break at midday. Once we are in our work mode, we are programmed to grind on until we are exhausted.

In rural Europe, the Angelus bells were rung at midday. It was a time for people in the fields to stop and realize that whatever they were doing was not the whole picture.

It feels good to pause during the day for a time of reflection. Today might be a good day to have a time when we remember that there is more to life than our work.

It is always refreshing to provide some breathing space in our lives when we can listen to a bird, or an angel, sing.

June 23
Life In A Different Key

I've always admired musicians, poets, and artists for the way that they are able to reshape the world in order to give a more authentic picture of life.

A musician can transpose a song from one key to another and change our ability to sing it. An artist can portray this world as being more than just what we see, but also what we feel. Arnold Steinhardt (1937 -), a famous and compassionate violinist, writes about life in a series entitled *In The Key of Strawberry*.

There are moments, often little ones I think, which can transpose our existence into a different spiritual key. It is good to take advantage of them.

JUNE 24
HAIKU BENCH

Do you know what's missing in your life and in my life? It is what my friend, the haiku poet and author, Cliff Edwards calls "moments of enlightenment during which we enter and share the life of even the smallest things around us." The older I get the more essential those moments become to a life of harmony and peace. At the same time, I have more difficulty in making space for them!

Guess what? I found a solution at a local hardware store. A small and simple black bench had been drastically cut in price. "Not very popular," the salesman told me. A practical *"moment of enlightenment"* jumped into my head and the bench was on its way home.

I call it a "haiku bench." No, it is not a magical place to produce haiku poems. But it has turned into a wonderful spot to have haiku moments —those times when I can really become aware of what is going on right around me and in the process lose my preoccupations for an important instant. Cliff Edwards describes this process to his college students as, *"a glimpse into the mystery of the universe which is at the same time a doorway into the meaning of your own life."*

June 25
Different Worlds

Perhaps we all live in at least four different worlds.

In the first, a world of objects, we must be able to see ourselves as a thing and respect the natural forces governing all things. More important, we must see the commonness between ourselves and other things.

The second world is one of roles. We function as parents, teachers, helpers or those who are asking for help. We see and even tend to judge ourselves by how well we function in these roles.

In the third world of "I and Thou" we see each other as people, as individuals. We do not have social roles and don't ask each other what we can do. I see myself in you and feel you in me.

The fourth, and further, worlds start out as the world of me. It is the most unfamiliar of all worlds. As children most of us truly experience our own inner world, but as we grow older we lose contact. But it is in the fourth world that we must journey as we struggle spiritually. In the fourth-plus worlds everything we have experienced evolves. It is an evolution of consciousness which becomes a gateway to all that has been, is, and will be.

At least, that is how it all feels to me.

June 26
Loving And Being Loved

Truly, there is love within each of us.

We long to make a joyful connection with every flower and animal around us. We also have love for people in our hearts. This love will turn into a hard lump unless we let it out.

Love is a two-way thing. We cannot love a flower unless we let the flower love us. Love is a mutual touching.

The Jewish philosopher Martin Buber (1878–1965) said the encounter of love was moving to meet that which is moving to meet us. The Catholic priest and paleontologist Teilhard de Chardin (1881–1953) saw this process as essential to the progression of human consciousness. It is, he wrote, *"the blood of spiritual evolution."*

Love is sometimes not easy but it is always worth the effort, for each of us and for the cosmos.

June 27
Be Still And Know

Trees surround me where I live. They are constantly telling me, as in Psalm 46, to *Be still and know.*

A tree knows where it is on nature's wheel. Whatever the situation—budding, in full leaf, with ripe fruit—it is all part of being a tree.

We each have seasons in our lives. I've often found that if I try to bear fruit when it is time to bud, then I don't bud!

Most days I try to listen to the song of nature, though I know it's sometimes hard with the constant push of modern life. But it's good to slow down sometimes and appreciate that every year is a cycle—there is a time for activity and a time for quiet. There are always moments of beginning and moments of ending. Seasons for moving and seasons for renewal.

Be still and know. Slow down and watch nature's story unfold — around us and within us.

June 28
Turning Home

One of the most important steps on the spiritual path for the average seeker can quite possibly be the decision to stop moving in the present direction. This is a basic and simple idea, but one that is often difficult to grasp.

Most of the life that we lead is spent frantically adding on—collecting tricks and shortcuts to momentarily take our attention away from the deep pain and longing we might feel.

Some may take opportunities to slow down, to listen to the voice of homesickness, to stop. The road home often requires an initial awakening and then a turning around. Once we start back there may be a number of steps, but the path leads to gaining a new perspective on life.

Something inside each of us is waiting to help point the way.

JUNE 29
A RHYTHM OF LIFE

There is a rhythm in all of life. One of the reasons I love living among the redwoods of California and the olive trees on our farm is because it affords many moments of quiet contemplation. And I've found that, for me, the rhythm of life can only really be heard in moments of quiet.

At first I might look outside myself, but only hear a faint sound. That's because when searching for the rhythm, usually I must listen *inside*. When I am in harmony with this rhythm there is a sense of completeness.

If you were to try this today, you might hear that song. But then you must decide what you will do. You can wander in search of other tunes. You can stand rigid and continue to listen. Or you can let the song possess you.

Each of us can become a part of the rhythm of life.

June 30
Searching For Flowers

When I was a child, before people walked on the moon, the cosmos was a simple three-layered affair. Heaven was above. Hell was below. At times fiery lava broke through and flowed onto the earth's surface—providing proof of what is under the thin crust on which the living dwell.

I am occasionally among those who wonder if our home is nothing more than the dome of Hades. There are no rational solutions to many of our afflictions. But a simple alternative concept is found in one of Issa's (1763–1828) poems,

In our pilgrimage across the roof of hell—
let us search for flowers.

In that search I have found some flowers. There are the people closest to me. There are people I have never met. There is the mystery I label "God." It is a breathtaking bouquet I'm collecting. Sometimes I am able to step back from my own concerns long enough to realize that every careworn creature with whom I share this moment in history is also searching for flowers.

That is our bond.

JULY

July 1
Where Is The Hay?

One morning in 1863, as the sunlight crept down the streets of Amherst, Massachusetts, Emily Dickinson (1830–1886) looked out of her upstairs bedroom window and demanded;

Answer July
Where is the Bee—
Where is the Blush—
Where is the Hay?

July is a very physical month, and the poet wanted those sounds, sights, and smells. People who have serious concerns about life and faith are admirable — I trust I am one of them. But, perhaps this is the month to lay those concerns aside and simply to be at home on the earth. Our world is alive and we should enjoy it for its own sake!

I was in Emily Dickinson's Amherst one July. Young professional musicians were gathering to play, not for professors or for career advantage, but purely for the love of music. Whenever they could find an hour, some musicians walked the countryside and sat on fences watching farmers practice their artistry. In the evening, the farmers were part of the audience listening to Bach, Beethoven, Brahms.

To me — working neither in the fields nor on stage — the man on the tractor and the young woman on the cello seemed part of the same community.

July 2
The Season Comes, The Season Goes

D ark English Lavender is on the east side of our chapel. It is beautiful, but it is the variety of lavender that is essential for the type of infused olive-oil balm that my sister Marti made from a small amount of our sister Julie's olive oil. It is also the lavender my daughter Holly dries, uses to decorate the house and weaves to be sold at our Christmas Faire. So every time I go to the chapel this patch of purple beauty has shrunk from the harvesting.

The bees and I are sad. But this is something we must learn from nature, that everything in life is provisional. We don't harvest the lighter-colored French Lavender from the West side of the chapel—partly because of my complaining. But, even in time there, the blossoms fade and drop.

As the Bible says; *"For everything there is a season,"* So we all just have to get used to it!

July 3
Simply Us

In the country there can be a precise time when weather and instinct come together and something has to be done — like haying. In years past this was the fundamental farm activity. Hay would fuel the horses and oxen. Cows convert the hay to milk from which come a host of other products. Without hay the fields would not be ploughed, the buggy pulled, the family fed.

My image of the best in our country is not dressing up in red, white and blue and barbequing under a sky filled with fireworks, but rather folks helping each other bring in the hay. These people in plain sweaty clothes saw the character of their neighbors as they worked together without concern for station or wealth. There was no "we" and "they" — simply "us."

When our family had cows here at home, we stored hay in our barn. We don't anymore and I miss it. Perhaps deep in all our psyches, urban and rural, is something still responding to the smell of new-mowed hay — and with it, a spirit of cooperation.

July 4
And Crown Thy Good With Brotherhood

People in the United States celebrate our independent spirit today. Parts of our history bother me but I still put out the flag on the 4th and enjoy a big picnic under an oak tree. We live in a wonderful land. Our story has great moments, magnificent heroes. I admire our revolution and the bold spirit of freshness that runs through our story. We have done quite well with keeping alive our spirit of independence. We have not been as successful in working for the common good.

There has always been a struggle to define the *"We"* in the Constitution's *"WE THE PEOPLE ...."* Does it include Native Peoples? Blacks? Religious non-conformists? Women? LGBTs? Immigrants? The poor? The sick?

I wish we would celebrate our compassion today. In these challenging many of our citizens feel alone. But of late, seeking a personal advantage and lending a helping hand are too often competing forces in matters large and small.

Our country is not only about coming in first. In the opening paragraph of the Constitution we also find our founders pledge to *"... promote the general Welfare ... ."* It was a practical necessity of life when our country was new.

It still is.

July 5
The Redcoats Are Here Again!

A war is still going on between myself and the Redcoats. The battleground is not the bridge on Concord, Massachusetts but two small guava trees. My foes are fanatical English robins. No muskets are fired but there is the frequent rapping of my walking stick on the window.

At this time of year, the little trees are covered with large red blossoms which, if left alone, will ripen into delicious fruit in November and December when such delicacies are greatly treasured around here. The problem is that the blossoms are, to birds, a narcotic! It is nice to see happy birds but every blossom they attack is one less guava for our table in autumn.

Our nation's founders were fighting for individual freedom from monarchial domination. They were very noble in that venture, and we continue the insistence on liberty. But, to be frank, we have never been enthusiastic about responsibility for the common good. Could it be that both the robins and I are part of the common community of nature and I should be thinking about our "general Welfare?" as it says in the U.S. Constitution? If so, does this call for a sense of partnership, rather than how can I control the situation for only my advantage?

That idea takes a bit of stretching. But...

JULY 6
IS IT ENOUGH TO BE?

This is a month when, at least in the rural countryside, everyone seems overwhelmed by tasks. I am only able to look on, more than I would like. Advanced years and the need to use a wheelchair at times can make me feel out of place. I grew up believing everyone has to have a task. It was not enough, for me at least, to just be. Yet I am fascinated by my little grandson Damien's ability to simply take joy in life itself!

Now what do I do? What divine instructions have been implanted in my spiritual genes that can be relied upon when days are good, as well as when they are challenging?

Well, there is always the task the psalmist sets forth for us all in Psalm 57: *Awake my soul, awake lyre and harp, I will awake the dawn!*

I think I will go do that...

July 7
Learning How To
Die And Live

At this time of year, surrounded by new life in nature, it is not uncommon for older folk like myself to cast thoughts forward to our final years. We are becoming aware that, as Leonardo da Vinci (1452–1519) put it, *"While I thought that I was learning how to live, I have been learning how to die."*

We often act as if we were immortal when we become involved with petty, selfish things. If we accept the fact that we will die, it may help us disengage from these entanglements and more humbly focus on the process of living.

Sometimes, when we are still for a moment, there comes an image of our last moments of life. The experience of that reflection can guide us in our response to now — this present moment.

July 8
Calm And Free

William Wordsworth (1770–1850) was a serious and cerebral poet who lived through dark times. He had an affair with a young French woman during the Revolution in 1792. A daughter, Caroline, was born.

Because of wars, Wordsworth didn't meet Caroline until she was 9. They took a walk on the beach at Calais on *"a beauteous evening, calm and free."* It was a moment of cosmic majesty for the poet. But for Caroline it was all simply being part of nature, of God being with this young girl in an ordinary way. Wordsworth was deeply impressed and wrote: *If thou appear untouched by solemn thought, / Thy nature is not therefore less divine.*

Sometimes it is good to remain untouched by solemn thought in order to enter more completely into the sacred experience that surrounds us.

July 9
Singing At Heavens Gate

One mid-summer, a vibrant flock of violinists, violists, and cellists – graduates from Boston, New York, and San Francisco conservatories – descended on our farm to take a breath before their incredibly busy late-summer performances.

When it seemed a new quartet might be forming, one member wanted "Lark" in the name. The Skylark — that wonderful little creature so often the subject of art, writing, and music. A quite dull looking bird, the Skylark scratches in grain fields generally unnoticed. However, when it is in flight, and only a dot in the sky, the bird sings a beautiful song for two or more minutes.

Many have marveled at this drab creature reserving its gift for the open sky. William Shakespeare (1564–1616) wrote: *"Like to the lark at break of day arising from sullen earth, sings hymns at heaven's gate."* The composer Ralph Vaughan Williams (1872–1958) gave to the violin the beautiful chirps, trills, and notes of the lark's song in *"The Lark Ascending."* At the end, the singing seems to go out of range, but we know it continues even if we cannot hear it.

I think we all have a special song to sing as we fly from "sullen earth" to "heaven's gate" — a song that comes naturally. When to sing? We do not have to worry about that. Our song, like that of the Skylark, will be fitting for any time and any day in our lives.

July 10
A Sacred Pot

Long ago Rabbi Nachman of Breslov (1772–1810) wrote;

*May it be my practice to go outdoors each day
among the trees and grasses, among all growing
things, there to be alone and enter into prayer.*

Where I live I am surrounded by "the trees and grasses"
Rabbi Nachman mentions. But I have become aware
that many with whom I share this planet do not have the
options with which I am blessed. It impresses me how even
though confined by sickness, poverty, or other circumstances, people do find ways to use nature as a connection
to what is sacred.

I have been in cramped rooms and noticed the care given
to a little pot with something growing in it. Sometimes
when I follow Rabbi Nachman's advice and go outdoors,
I do not head for my usual beautiful spots; in the rose
garden, on the edge of the forest, overlooking an olive
grove. Instead I sit on the steps next to a small potted gera-
nium my daughter Holly gave to me when I was a bit under

the weather. In that pot I am learning to find everything needed to remind me of what is holy in me, in you, in life.

And memories come flooding in of sitting next to a potted plant as a very young child in the hot Mississippi sun, or on my desk in my law office, or in the corner of a dank concrete Romanian building at a very bad time. And looking forward, I know there will be times when only a small piece of the wonderful life growing on this planet will be all that connects me to what is important. But that little piece will be enough.

July 11
Nothing Special

Standing at the bend of a river I can understand why spiritual guides of East and West are fascinated by water.

To be humble is to be like water. Water flows into low places. The Chinese Tao says;

The highest good is like water. For water benefits the 10,000 things without striving. It settles in places that people avoid...

And on the other side of the planet the Shakers sing; *"Down in the lowly vale, living waters never fail"*

Water is soft and yet can overcome the hardest stone. It is beautiful and yet is nothing special.

I guess the point is to give up being special. Be common. Be as common as a field of flowers on a summer afternoon. To experience our commonness can be rich. As rich as water at the bend of a river.

July 12
When Past Is Present

Sometimes I stand in a place and know that once something very important happened here. This is a place where people or just a solitary person lived out a dream. Maybe it was something that changed the course of history or just impacted deeply one individual being. But what is truly authentic, no matter how small or how big, in some way remains forever.

Our ancestors were once rooted to the ground of their birthplace. This connection has largely disappeared for most of us, but the earth itself can still be an anchor. A friend told me that when his mother died he laid on the ground with his arms and legs spread out to feel the comfort it offered.

Each patch of earth has its own story, and holds the stories of the lives it has supported —including our own.

JULY 13
GOD'S BREATH

On a warm summer day, I often find myself waiting for a breeze — a refreshing breath from heaven. Our word "spiritual" derives from the Latin *spirare*, meaning to breathe or blow. *Spirare* also describes the animating agent that gives life to creatures and is sometimes translated simply as "the breath of life."

Many languages have words that imitate breath: *chi* in Chinese, *psyche* in Greek. The fact that there was an actual sound connected with the spiritual suggests it was quite real to the ancients.

While religious teachings may offer us a possible under-standings of existence, what we truly hunger for is the actual experience of the breath of life. Like a gentle breeze on a hot day. For, as Job learned in the midst of his great trials (33:4),

It is God's breath that gives me life.

July 14
The Planet Of The
Vulnerable

A gentle friend of mine has been diagnosed with melanoma. After a recent surgery, a companion said to my friend, "Welcome to the planet of the vulnerable!"

Years ago I was visiting the Hopi region in the arid plateaus of Northeastern Arizona. My guide was a Kachina doll carver. He lived on a high mesa, and had a corn field at the base of the hill. One evening I walked out in the field. It was late July and the corn was only about 10 inches high. There was no irrigation system and no rain in the forecast. The situation did not seem very promising to me. Corn was an essential Hopi staple. Talk about vulnerable!

"Hopi" means "People of Peace." They call their corn, which was given them by a divine spirit, the "Mother of Life." It must be planted with a good heart. Everything about the cultivation teaches us about spiritual growth. Facilitating the growth of corn and raising children is very much the same for the Hopi. A meal is made from the corn to use through the winter and at ceremonial times, such as important steps in life, much the same as incense is employed in the solemn liturgies of various religions.

Well, if the corn is so important why not dig wells and build irrigation systems? That is not how it works. To me, the Hopi lands are at the center of "the planet of the vulnerable." I think the Hopi would agree with my friend when she says her vulnerability results in being open "to finding love and support and ways to be grateful."

JULY 15
A SUMMER CANTICLE

For me, and those with whom I live, singing is one of the ways to be grateful — to build a bridge between any aspect of our existence, including a corn field, and the sacred harmony of creation. We fused together some Hopi texts to have this song, a psalm of Kachina spirits:

In the summertime we will come again. We will come as clouds from the west, the south, the east and the north to bless the people of peace and to water their fields and crops. Then the people of peace will see their corn plants majestically growing. They will be happy and they will joyfully sing praises to the spiritual beings who brought moisture.

At the edge of the cornfield a bird will sing with them in the oneness of their happiness. So they will sing together in tune with the universal power, in harmony with the one creator of all things.

July 16
Before Dawn

The days had been hot. I woke up about 3 AM and stepped outside. A sweet breeze was cooling the land.

All those biblical references to God being found not in storms and earthquakes but in the gentle breeze came to mind. When we are young that breeze is a compass leading us through the challenging thicket of life to a path of compassion. No matter how our religious and social beliefs change with age, that compass seems to be constantly pointing to love.

For those of us who are old, the breeze may seem stronger. It is as if we are now in a clearing, and sacred comfort can be found where we stand, not so much by what we are doing, but by our simply being. At least, that is how it is at 3 o'clock in the morning.

July 17
Soup

Mid-summer and I am surrounded by a garden of food. However, poverty also surrounds me. I just don't see it. One in eight people on earth goes to bed hungry. I am not one of them, but, being born in the Great Depression, I learned from my parents that I can find part of the solution to world hunger on the street where I live.

My mother knew the condition of every household on our street. She made soup every day I can recall — enough for us and for some neighbors as well. Poverty was no disgrace. We gave when we could and neighbors accepted without embarrassment because it was the right thing to do. We all recognized the need for finding common ground. That need is greater than ever today, as the distinction between my street and my planet is diminishing.

We can all help combat that soul-sucking feeling of people facing bad times alone. We should look for neighbors in material or emotional need and push right in with a helping hand. And, not be reluctant to ask when we need it ourselves.

Helping each other helps us all.

JULY 18
WHOA!

I get caught in rush hour traffic. I can't find a parking place in the college lot. I'm racing down the hall when the bell rings. I'm supposed to be giving a guest lecture on spirituality to 200 waiting psychology students. Suddenly my friend, the professor Gordon Tappan, jumps in front of me like a football linesman, grabs my shoulders and shouts, "STOP! NOW BREATHE!"

OK. If that is all you need to hear to stop the faster-and-faster bullet train of your life, and step off and enjoy the quiet and peaceful countryside, then just stop reading and stop the darn train. And whenever you find yourself on that train again: remember this image of Gordon or anyone else you admire jumping in front of you and shouting, "STOP! NOW BREATHE!"

Do that a couple of dozen times a day and it will work wonders.

July 19
A Time to Grow

Everything growing around me seems to know where it is going. What about us humans? We, with heavens help, are to bring about the longed-for peaceful kingdom. How? We must become fully human persons whose depths are divine.

In order to show us how this can be done, heavenly beings occasionally come among us, not as supernatural creatures but as humble working women and men. Take Jesus, for example. He was a fellow human being who demonstrated by his own life that spiritual growth was to be sought not outside our daily sorrow and joys, but in their very midst. He was not less human than most of us. He was more human.

How do we become fully human? By growing in love through caring for and healing each other.

JULY 20
ENCOUNTER

I think it was Martin Buber (1878–1965) who urged us to frequently contemplate the wonder of an authentic relationship — where I am moving to meet someone who is moving to meet me.

If I can be a person for others and find something sacred in others as well as in myself, then I can dance around the universe with another human being doing the same thing.

It is a bond I cannot control. I am vulnerable, and perhaps afraid, as I encounter someone who is encountering me. However, as a result, I lose my separateness and become more fully human.

It is the most nourishing relationship I can have with another person — and perhaps with the universe.

Worth thinking about.

JULY 21
SOFIA

Mid-July and we have an abundance of food in the garden and orchard. Apples fall and rabbits come to nibble. This day, I am in a wheelchair at a food pantry we provide. I interrupt a daydream to find I am eye-to-eye with the future in the person of a very serious 8-year-old who asks me: "Did you ever trap a bear?"

I recognize Sofia as a third-grader at the local school. She is a good student from a hard working Latino family. Except that work of any kind is hard to find this summer. Sofia could have asked a much more difficult question — like why do some of her cousins go to bed hungry in this rich country. I read recently where some guy set the world record by eating 69 hot dogs and became a local hero. This afternoon we are running low on food to distribute, what does that make us — losers?

Sofia did ask about the wheelchair and I said at the moment my legs were not working well. She said she had a cousin whose legs did not work, but he did not have a chair with wheels. I said I was sorry. She said, "That's OK."

There she stood, this girl who, if not prevented, will inherit the earth. She has a steady gaze and many more serious questions beginning to form behind those eyes. If we as a nation continue to be so timid in defining the human tribe, Sofia may well become a rebel helping society do what is right. As for now, she is a little girl and I am an old man. Tonight we will both have enough to eat.

July 22
Reflections On A Seed

Many ages ago a seed became a flower. That flower produced seeds. The seeds grew into flowers. Each flower we look at today is part of a solid line of existence going back to the beginning of life. Each flower needs every flower and seed that has gone before it.

Each of us is a flower and a seed. We are each part of a story which began with the first cell of life. That story will continue on after us. The many people and things we have each touched in our life will be influenced by us. The history of the world would not be the same if you and I had not been here. The small ripples we cause today may bring huge waves in ages to come.

July 23
Watching The Margins

In the corner of our little rose garden are two clumps of a variety of Spanish Lavender, which seem drab compared to their cousins near the chapel; the dark English Lavender on the east side and the French Lavender on the west.

The Spanish Lavender is not as charming to look at, long green stalks with a few light purple blossoms. But it will remain unchanged for many weeks long after the others are bloomed out.

In life, there is always something to be found on the margins which is somehow out of step but still a gateway to memories and to hopes for the future.

JULY 24
THE GARDEN AS SACRAMENT

Beauty is not a luxury but a precondition. Generations of Japanese poets and painters have known the necessity of a place between the inner experience and the outer world. In our youth and in old age, we live primarily in this "garden" at important times.

For me, that place is increasingly an actual little garden. Once I was to have a brief contact with an old friend who was only days from death. I was not sure how to use that brief time. I went into the garden to think about it. A hummingbird zoomed past me and connected with a tiny red flower. It happened several times. I realized this is what I wanted to share with my friend. It was the right thing to do. Since that time I have looked for the answer to many nagging questions looking at a rose or a violet.

Nature is something which brings us pleasure. But it does more than that, it takes us beyond the daily grind and therefore helps us gain perspective, refreshes our spirit, helps us find more meaning in life, and gives us a sense of wholeness.

July 25
Something Forgotten
In The Old House

Jesus of Nazareth is a bridge between the divine and the human, but many people are tired of hearing about Jesus. The American author Walker Percy (1916–1990) observed that the Christian- Catholic novelist was like a person *"who has found a treasure hidden in the attic of an old house but he is writing for people who have moved out to the suburbs and who are bloody sick of the old house and everything in it."* Percy was concerned about the despair born of the rootlessness of people in contemporary society. He wanted us to get up in that attic and rediscover our treasures. That means we have to ignore a lot of shallow references to Jesus in the media and in pulpits.

In each generation, the greatest obstacle to a person becoming a follower of Jesus has been encountering self-righteous Christians. It is helpful to remember that Jesus himself was not a Christian. He was an unschooled Jewish layman who ignored established religious traditions and institutions.

The "good news" he brought was that everyone can have hope, because human well-being is the keystone in God's plan of salvation, and that plan is universal. It includes everyone.

How is the plan realized? If we transcend our fears and our self-interest, we can together make the kingdom of God a reality on earth.

July 26
As the World Sleeps

When the days are very hot we don't open our windows until there is a cool breeze during the night. These same days are times of heavy work for others in our little community, and they need their rest. So it is often my delightful task to stumble about during the night hours opening some of the windows.

This reminds me, and any of you who find yourself up in the hours of the night, to performing the task of monks through the ages who would arise at night to pray on behalf of the sleeping world. Often I find myself remembering, and occasionally reciting, the opening phrase of the nocturnal service of Vigils which translates something like,

"Lord, open my lips and my mouth shall proclaim your praise."

To me, there are several unique things about contemplation at night, be it opening windows or sitting beside the sickbed of someone we love, or just being awake for no apparent reason. We transcend our personal preoccupations.

In these quiet hours, we sense our connection to all of humanity; those in fear, mourning, struggling as refugees, hungry, laboring under the burdens of being young —or old —or alone. The curtains separating us from others seem to part, one after another.

I am not really alone as I open the windows and feel the breeze. There is the sleepy-eyed cat at the end of the hall patiently waiting for me to remember that nighttime is for sleeping. And, most important, there is the frog in the rose garden who is tonight's cantor as he intones his version of:

"... *Lord, open my lips and my mouth shall proclaim your praise.*"

July 27
Memories Of Grass
And Hay

To help transcend our preoccupations, we can sometimes focus on simple objects, and somehow come to a broader horizon in life. I often use music or looking at the stars, or very common things close at hand: a tree, a picture, a cloud, a candle flame. This time of year there is always grass.

The younger folk, human and animal, glide through the tall grass as if they were swimming. The rest of us sit and reflect.

When my family had a few cows we kept an old barn full of hay. Those who shared an experience like that know how special it was to enter the quiet and cool space and be almost overcome by the fragrance of the hay. For me, it was sweeter than the lingering smell of incense in a cathedral.

For most of us those days are largely gone but doesn't something of that memory come back as we mow the lawn or sit in a field and watch the wild oats ripen?

JULY 28
CARE AND COMFORT

"Care" has been in the English language a long time. The Old Saxon root of "care" is *kara*, which is the word for "lament." As early as A.D. 725 the word "care" was used in *Beowulf*. But "carefree" did not appear until about 1800. Attempting to live without care is a decidedly modern folly.

Every person experiences severe troubles—things she or he would have done anything to avoid. But to be human is to sometimes journey over rough terrain. I cannot avoid the troubles of living. Yet I can choose how I respond to them. I am the only one who can destroy my life with fears and poisonous anger. I must realize that I need help at such times, and that the help is always there if I turn from my preoccupations and compulsions long enough to be mindful of the solace offered.

I am not in this journey alone. There is grace around me — from Providence, from people, from nature, from the story of life itself, from the unknown. If you are like me, you have to be reminded of that blessing from time-to-time.

July 29
And Then There
Was A Bee

Once when I had the most wonderful idea for an essay on summertime, a bee flew across my desk. This was a very loud bee, and it kept flying back and forth and driving all the beautiful thoughts out of my mind.

It was an intolerable situation. I mean, this bee was extremely loud. I noticed he was also quite large. One of an army of drones no doubt. It wasn't like he was the Queen or something special. He was just an annoying distraction. I went searching for a fly swatter. And when armed, I found him taking a rest on my window. An easy target!

As I swung back with the swatter, a troubling thought came into my head. Is there common ground here? I want him gone and he wants to be gone. This is silly, that I am stopping my creative work to consider liberating a bee!

Anyway, I emptied a plastic paper clip container and put it over the bee. He took to it right away. Some relief from his frustration I suppose. I slipped a piece of paper between the container and the window and carefully turned it over. He was surprisingly calm. I walked to the door and pushed it open. As soon as I removed the paper, the bee took off with amazing speed and in a straight line to some apparently specific destination. He never had any doubt about where he was going. Immediately he was out of sight!

I was left standing in the doorway with an empty paperclip container in one hand and a piece of paper in the other, and not quite remembering what I was going to write about summer.

JULY 30
BE YOURSELF, THAT IS WHO YOU WERE MEANT TO BE!

Here I am, sitting in a little park and collecting my thoughts before giving a talk. It is feeding time, and the various waterfowl enthusiastically join in the evening ritual. Except for the swans. They float by majestically. Somehow there is always some food near them which they gracefully pick out of the water. I remember a line from something I read many years ago from an ancient Chinese sage about a swan, or perhaps it was a snow goose or some other white bird. *The swan need not bathe to make itself white. Neither need you do anything but be yourself.*

Being myself is a very difficult task. Here am I sitting and contemplating how I can become somebody else for the evening; a great writer, a remarkable spiritual guide, a humble hero, a brilliant thinker, the most inspiring speaker anyone ever listened to. That is all very impressive, but it is not being myself, is it?

Perhaps the real process of emotional and spiritual growth must always begin by being ourselves, no matter what that means. It is not easy. But at least tonight I'm going to give it a try!

Time to get up and go to the gathering. But first a slight bow to the naturally white swans.

July 31
The Waves in Life

The last day of a month filled with so much blooming and growing. With some reluctance, I turn the calendar page. But every single moment is both an ending and a beginning.

This present second could see the end of all. This instant could be a new beginning for all. If we really jump into what medieval mystics sometimes called "the now-moment," we might well be completely renewed!

Life, like an ocean, is made up of many waves. There are waves for each moment, each day, each year, each life. If we hunger after a sense of completeness, we must be in harmony with the waves.

Now, on to August!

AUGUST

AUGUST 1
LAMMASTIDE

Have you ever stepped into an ancient building or stood on the edge of a natural site and felt that you had some connection with that space? I have. It is as if there is something in my cultural DNA that connects me. That is how I feel about Lammastide — the beginning of August.

This is the time for the wheat harvest. It was the first harvest of crops necessary to sustain life through the winter. It also signaled a significant change in the seasons. August is not just a continuation of the summer; it is when we begin to harvest.

This is an old pre-Christian festival carried over into Christian times. "Lammas" breaks down into the "Mass of the loaf". Every family baked a loaf of bread from the new wheat and took it to the village church. In some places there was a great festival, and people rode to the church atop the harvest wagons in a celebration known as "Harvest Home."

A person living close to the land will feel a change in the tempo of the season. It was understood that at this time we all help each other, for nothing was as important as the harvest. There is a role I must fulfill together with others to harvest what has been planted and cared for. That is true not only of the land but also in my own life and in the society in which I live.

AUGUST 2
A TIME TO COME TOGETHER

These days are important bridges in nature's cycle. Often I am slow in understanding that August is not simply the end of a season but a unique and brief time of transition. Gradually, I do become mindful of tinges of color in the trees and ripened fruits in the orchard.

Years ago, this was a time when everything stopped. All people, no matter what their station in life, turned out to bring in the harvest before some disaster struck. Artists painted the activity. Poets wrote of it. Composers captured in music the essence of life in these few weeks.

My experience is different from most of the countless farmers who have worked the land through the centuries. None of my neighbors are out harvesting grain. We all buy our flour in a store. But there are similarities. Here in Sonoma County, California, the beginning of the grape harvest is what provides the beat of life on much of the land. The new bread at harvest time and the new wine run together in my thinking — elements long held sacred in many cultures.

AUGUST 3
STORM CLOUDS

In medieval agriculture the grain harvest was a time filled with apprehension, because despite all the effort that went into planning, planting, and caring, a sudden storm could destroy the crop. This would lead to a hungry winter with little bread.

Shakespeare and other writers pointed out that this was also a time to care for our emotional and spiritual growth. Juliet was born the night before Lammastide. She died hours before her 14th birthday and was never to enjoy the harvest of her love for Romeo. Storm clouds are a threat to our plans at any age. This is a time to be grounded and connected to what matters to us.

We and neighbors around us are gathering harvests from gardens and the wild to store up for the winter. And, whether we are 14 or 114, these days before autumn are very important for taking stock of where we have been and where we want to go, especially if the world around us is changing — as it always is.

AUGUST 4
GLEANING

In the early days of our country, following European tradition, August was understood to be a month of charity as required in the Hebrew Bible (Leviticus 19: 9–10):

> *When you gather the harvest of your land, you are not to harvest to the very end of the field. You are not to harvest the gleanings of the harvest. You are neither to strip your vine bare nor to collect the fruit that has fallen in your vineyard. You must leave them for the poor and the stranger.*

A small corner, open to the road, was often left after harvest where the needy could move into the field or orchard and glean. Today where I live, we and many others glean and contribute to Food Pantries and, in other ways, share the harvest with those who need it.

At the same time, there are many who walk the countryside seeking inner solace this month. They are also gleaners. They may be strangers to the overall nourishment of country life, but in August we are all gleaners of the comfort that comes from the land, a succor that is difficult to capture in words.

AUGUST 5
LETTING GO

My sister Marti wrote this haiku while living with pancreatic cancer: "

The old apple tree
bent branches heavy with fruit—
ready to let go."

During the AIDS pandemic and at other times, it has been my privilege to witness people who beautified the world in some way while facing their own serious troubles. I don't think it's a unique experience. What's the process? I'm not sure, but I think it goes something like this.

As all the things that we thought were important and we invested our energy in maintaining start stripping away, we begin to discover who we really are. The author and AIDS activist Paul Monette (1945–1995) was a close friend. On his tombstone he had it written "KNOW YOURSELF."

When we no longer are the roles we have played in life, when we throw away the masks we have worn, when we discover who we are essentially, when we know ourselves, when we let go, we can harvest every rich and beautiful thing from our life. Somehow, even when not intended, that harvest gets shared with a circle, which is sometimes little and sometimes very big.

August 6
On The Wings Of Birds

At this time of year, when we here are harvesting in the orchard and garden, it is natural to be aware that all of life is in a process of constant change. There is a sense of the sacred about the land on which any of us live. Here that is marked by memories of spots where beautiful things have and are happening; the chapel, the cemeteries, and the olive groves which invite reflection, the places where the children play—and sometimes pray.

Soon nature's great wheel will once again begin to turn from summer to autumn. On our farm, the birds will remind us of this. The swallows, who came in March to nest, will circle next month until it is clear that all the young ones can fly. Then they will be off on the long trip to South America. Not long after that, other little birds will arrive from the North and settle down until spring.

Whatever the seasonal changes, there is always the sound of birds — and the winds of the spirit.

August 7
The Last Chapter

Stacking wood brings thoughts of cozy fires to come, but also the realization that this wood came from a tree that grew old, fell, and was cut up. Death and endings are a part of August. The grain is cut. That can be a very painful and jarring experience when carried over into personal life.

The process of life and death is clear. All things, including humans, grow and die, leaving seeds for the future. The wheel of life turns. It makes sense from the outside. It hurts when we are on the inside. There are many uncertainties. Questions we hear from dying friends are poignant and indelible. When he knew he did not have much time to live my friend Red asked me, "How do I get through this last chapter?" We talked and I left knowing that question would never leave me until it was my question.

Ultimately, no one withstands time. My life will one day be harvested, perhaps soon. But, I tell myself, "You are not dying now. So get on with living."

August 8
Finding the Sacred

There are many ways in which I have experienced a sacred reality.

I have found it in the silences and in thoughts and words I sometimes label "prayer" and "meditation." I also find that same reality in nature, history, and in the cycles and changes of life, years, and days.

Increasingly, I am also aware of the sacred in people. Many spiritual traditions recognize there is something blessed in every person. In Hinduism the customary greeting, "Namaste", roughly means "I bow to the divine in you." Mother Teresa of Calcutta (1910–1997) told her Sisters if they were searching for Jesus they would find him in the eyes of the person they were facing.

There are many ways of saying there is something sacred in every person.

August 9
The Faith of Small
Creatures

Sitting on a familiar bench, I can gaze out to forested hills on the far horizon. But I find myself primarily looking down — the world at my feet, where some wise Rabbi directed those to look who wanted to discover the face of God. I find little insects. These small creatures are going about the same tasks their ancestors have been performing for centuries or longer. As far as I can tell they know what they are doing and how to do it. That's where my problem comes in.

At this moment in history the human world is, in my opinion, in a horrible mess, much of it brought about by feelings of deep disappointment and isolation. It used to be that when someone my age expressed thoughts like these, the younger generation would roll their eyes and go back to their iPods. Not so much now, as the financial gap widens between the privileged few and the growing number who see their dreams fading away.

But our human world is not the only world. And perhaps at these times we can find some wisdom in observing the other circles of existence on this planet which is home to us all.

Regrets and fear are the two great obstacles to finding a sanctuary of peace in my heart. But living completely without regret or fear, these creatures at my feet seem to have a stronger faith than I do about existence — being where I ought to be, doing what I ought to do, feeling at home on the earth, and in this present moment. I think I am beginning to better understand what the wise Rabbi meant about looking down to find the face of God!

August 10
The Corn Row

When I was very young I heard my father say that he liked to sit on the porch in the evening and listen to the corn grow. I tried it a couple of times and didn't hear anything. But, the quiet was nice and I did think I could smell the corn.

Later when I was a teenager and worked in a cannery, I learned that the scent of corn can carry quite a distance. The smell and the memories come back now as I walk down the rows of corn in our garden. I hear and imagine things I do not understand.

Labyrinths as spiritual tools are rather popular at the moment. One author, borrowing from a number of cultures, views pregnancy as our first experience of a labyrinth. Can this row of corn become a labyrinth with me on one end and a grandchild-to-be on the other? It's going to take a little imagining. Here am I, slowly going down this long row of corn with a lot of life and experience behind me. In my mind's eye, I try to make out a small but ever-growing child coming toward me. Suppose we stop when we meet each other, and the child asks, "What should I know about where you have been and where I am going?"

It is worth thinking about!

AUGUST 11
HARVEST JOYS

At my home and across the country, gardens and orchards are in full harvest.

For us, apples and tomatoes are setting the pace. I wake up to the smell of apple butter in the making. In the barn, fresh cider is being pressed. With the help of friends, old and new, the kitchen has become a production center for tomatoes and applesauce being canned for the winter. Meals these days are pretty much all things we have grown. The pumpkin patch I am growing for kids who come to our food pantry is stretching out and showing its strength. And there is much more to come!

With each thing I gather in the basket, I think of my own life and that of others. What have we grown in our hearts? What can we harvest?

AUGUST 12
HOLY DOUBT

A Buddhist student was once advised that to travel the sacred path three virtues were required: great courage, great faith, and great doubt.

In the western world we have appreciated courage and honored martyrs. The valor of early Christians attracted many followers. Faith is given much lip service. If "faith" meant "belief" then the many creeds we have developed would be ample proof of faith.

However, a living faith cannot be a creed of words, but a person's whole response to a divine rhythm. In order to make that response we must accept the spiritual necessity of doubt.

Historically, doubt has been one of Christianity's weakest points. There has been an incredible insistence on certainty. What is frequently termed "a faith crisis" is usually a "holy doubt."

The only true crisis of faith is the refusal to struggle out of the religious cocoon in which we first gained an image of God, ourselves, and creation.

AUGUST 13
LISTENING TO THE STARS

My thoughts go back to an evening almost half a century ago. We were still in San Francisco and building bridges for ourselves and others between spiritual growth and various paths of psychology, Asian traditions, Christian mysticism, and all manner of things.

Sister Marti was giving a talk. She mentioned an author's reflection on how easy it is for us to lose what he called "the first things" concerning the adventure of existence. Marti was asked what was an example of one of those "first things" for her. She immediately responded,

> *"I think of the stars. Living in a universe with the stars. Being part of the same process and knowing it."*

There were tears in her eyes. Everyone in the room had a sense that we had just moved to a very deep level. But it was also a simple level, which Marti demonstrated in how she closed the meeting with the prayer she shared each night with the neglected toddlers she cared for at that time:

The night has come. The sun has gone down. The stars are out, the moon is out. The birds are in the trees. The little creatures are in their nests and holes. The cows are in the barns. The children are going to bed and everything is quiet. Let us be still and listen to the stars.

That is worth doing tonight!

AUGUST 14
JUST A PERSON

Several years ago I was deeply impressed by a well-known and respected physician who was having serious complications from brain tumors. Someone was trying to introduce him during a concert reception. He put out his hand and stopped her. Then, turning to the stranger, he said, *"I am just a man."*

As with most other people, it has been very important for me to find meaning in life. I've traveled through many crossroads. Looking back, I realize that the paths I have taken which I most value have led me from complexity to simplicity. In the process, I often become more vulnerable. However, if I don't put obstacles in my own path, I can now more fully find meaning in my existence.

But what about the future? Well, Jesus was right on when he said, *"Do not worry about tomorrow, it will take care of itself."* (Mt. 6:24). Musicians and artists will keep on bringing beauty to life, those I love will keep on nudging the world in healthy directions, some folks far away will be inspired to attempt wonderful things, the trees around me will keep on doing their breathtaking thing, and cats will keep on purring and napping. As for me, I hope I will become increasingly comfortable saying, *I am just a person — a note in the song of life.*

AUGUST 15
VIGILS

Saint Benedict's (480–547) Rule for Monastics has served through the centuries to the present day as a guideline for many spiritual communities, including our own little venture at Starcross. What Benedict wrote down was a compilation of many spiritual roadmaps of contemplatives who had gone before him. One common theme was the importance of a time of night prayer. This was often called "Vigils." And it is a good thing to consider for all searching people regardless of the spiritual path they are following.

An interesting aspect of Vigils is the lack of "spiritual materialism", meaning the predisposition in Christianity to pray FOR something; eternal salvation, good health, business prosperity, etc. In contrast, for many, Vigils has always been praying on behalf of all those who are asleep.

Most people need their sleep. It is absolutely essential if a person is working, parenting, caring for their own and others' health. The thinking goes that there are very few people who have the luxury to pray at night, and it should not be for personal gain but on behalf of the whole community of life.

One of the advantages of growing in years is that a person is often up at night. So why not open ourselves to the experience?

AUGUST 16
10,000 DOORS

Different people are going to pray in different ways and, as a result, there are many varieties of prayer. There is never one way that is best for all. It is said the Buddha announced there were 10,000 doors to meditation.

Many powerful personal and cultural influences are at work in the evolution of our spirituality. Choices in meditation and prayer depend more upon personal psychological inclinations, spiritual preferences, and cultural conditioning than on a person's theology.

The shape of the doors we use can explain differing prayer and meditation experiences. I can throw open great cathedral doors and see the light through stained glass. My neighbor sees the morning light through a crack in a broken window. There is only one sun, but the shape of our life experiences determines our awareness and understanding of what we see.

AUGUST 17
THE GOD QUESTION

The question of God for most adults is usually "Who is God?" or "What is God?" A child frequently asks "Where is God?", which is a more productive question, but still a difficult one.

I've often found that being honest with ourselves about how we already answer these questions is the beginning of a quest for the sacred, not the end of it. For many, the statement "I can't believe in God" merely means an unwillingness to accept the shallow understandings of the divine touted by all manner of dogmatic "true-believers" and equally dogmatic "true-non-believers." A philosopher once observed that rigid atheism and rigid theism are two sides of the same coin.

The troublesome question of "God" faces each of us. And it does take mountains of courage to explore the question of "God?" deeply throughout our lives — knowing there will never be a complete answer.

August 18
Life As Sacrament

All faith traditions acknowledge milestones in the journey of life: birth, maturity, partnership, death.

In the medieval Christian world, this acknowledgment was conveyed through the seven sacraments. In baptism, the infant was claimed for God. Penance let the sinner be reconciled with God. The young person was strengthened in confirmation. Matrimony or holy orders sanctified a vocation. Anointing helped the afflicted transcend sickness and pain, especially in the face of death. The Eucharist was a means for a group to gather, giving praise and thanks to God.

The seven sacraments are a neat and systemic way of viewing sacred reality. But manifestation of the divine in time and in space cannot be confined forever in a medieval theological box. Ralph Waldo Emerson (1803–1882) wrote, *"To the poet, to the philosopher, to the saint, all things are friendly and sacred, all events profitable, all days holy, all [of us] divine."*

Perhaps today is a milestone for you or me—a way to commemorate our past or take a step toward our future. Today let us find the presence of God in all aspects of life.

AUGUST 19
BEFORE THE END OF
AUGUST

O n the farm, these are busy days. But some time before the end of August, we have to acknowledge that these unique days are passing. In my youth, school opening was tied to crop harvesting. Young people were an invaluable part of that process. But now many schools open in late August.

When my own children were young, we found a time in August to go back to some favorite place in the mountains. Our destination was usually by a mountain river. As we climbed from the hot valley floor, the air of the foothills was cleaner and cooler. Autumn was already coming up there.

As the years rolled on and school kids became young adults, the talk gradually turned to career, college, or conservatory. But I could still hear the echoes from many years before as they prepared to take those first courageous steps into grade school.

One year, not long ago, we unpacked our lunch near a fast but shallow river, racing over a bed of lava rock. When we arrived, three young girls were enjoying a last just-before-school-begins dip. Leaves on the overhanging trees were turning color, dropping, and floating on the river that was flowing on as it has for centuries.

Now, that I am in my mid-80s, the childhood years of those children, and of my own children, form a montage that drifts often in my imagination.

AUGUST 20
WALL AS BRIDGE

During the AIDS pandemic, my sister Julie and I once took a pilgrimage to Assisi, the city of St. Francis, on our way back from Romania. It was during a very troubled time in both our lives. We stayed near the basilica dedicated to Francis's extraordinary disciple Clare, or "Chiara" as she was known by her townspeople. Early on the first morning, we walked to Santa Chiara.

The church's alternating layers of rose and white marble glistened in the soft morning light. By contrast the cavernous interior was dark and still. A few worshipers were gathering in a side chapel for Mass. We joined them. The sound of the priest's voice drew my attention. I turned toward the altar. There was no priest in sight. A woman sang a beautiful high pitched response. A choir took up the lilting chant. They were nowhere to be seen. The nuns and their priest were on the other side of the wall behind the empty altar. Unseen, but heard, the ancient morning drama was unfolding as it had for over seven hundred years.

This marginalized relationship to the ritual was oddly comforting to me at the time. Relations with the institutional church had become troublesome to me. Here in this motherhouse of one of the most traditional religious orders, I would have expected to be struck by the differences that divided me from the nuns. Instead I was conscious of what bound us together.

The wall between us was in fact a bridge.

AUGUST 21
NOT FAMOUS BUT NEEDED

At this time of year, when I find that I am just one of a group clipping beans for freezing or picking apples for the food pantry, I do occasionally have the embarrassing realization that I am never going to be a famous person.

I am in my mid-80s and if it hasn't happened yet it's not going to! Ushers do not make a fuss over me. Reporters do not call up and ask for my reactions to events of the day. My obituary will not be featured in the New York Times. No school will be named after me.

I would be very surprised if anyone over 50 has not had similar thoughts! But be of good cheer, famous or not, we have all been needed.

AUGUST 22
DRAGONFLY

I am very fond of a haiku by Issa (1763–1828),

I see far-off mountains
in the jeweled eyes
of the dragonfly!

Where I live, the dragonflies are beginning to show up. The black ones seem to come first. They cut through the air like travelers from some distant place and suddenly hover right before my face attempting to comprehend in a few seconds me and my story. Then they are off again, but it seems as if they have packed away something of the essence of each of us.

Issa is correct. As I was cutting the 358th bean for freezing and putting away for winter, I looked into a dragonfly's giant jeweled eyes and I really did see reflected "far-off mountains" and I knew I had walked in those places — and so have you.

We have each lived out stories that are unique and yet they weave beautifully into the pattern of universal life.

August 23
Unexpected Things

A few days ago, I had a midnight ride to the nearest Emergency Room about an hour's drive away. It was a much worse than usual attack of my old companion diverticulitis. There was an excellent and caring staff. However, unexpected things either in our personal lives or in our society can be very troubling. I can hear my Buddhist friends saying "they shouldn't be" — but they are.

The next day at home, I looked out a window and saw a cat I had never seen before. He was getting along alright until he saw me. I scribbled down,

Strange cat, frightened eyes—
"What will the next moment bring?"
he seems to wonder.

A few hours later I realized that the cat and I were one. As I lay there recuperating, I was certainly wondering, "What will the next moment bring?" My friend Cliff Edwards has often reminded us, "*The haiku becomes a doorway into the meaning of the here and now, and so a doorway into the meaning of our own life.*"

As I listened to the murmur of dearly beloved voices nearby going about our daily life, I realized that I often hold myself back from entering that doorway into the meaning of my life. It is that I try to control my own future. Finding the meaning of my life and attempting to control my life simply are things that do not go together.

August 24
Living With Uncertainty

Most of us have been hurt in some way, and we do not like risk. However, we must somehow find the encouragement to risk, and by risking, free the great creative energy within us.

We must learn to live with uncertainty. It was our natural condition in the caves. Living in such a situation calls forth our strength and our vitality. The demand for, and worse yet the finding of, a supposed security often heralds our destruction.

In moments of crisis, people often go in search of certainty, be it the certainty of a god, a devil, a spirit, a science, an institution, or a theory. Whatever a person's certainty, he or she will find evidence to support it. However, our hope lies in the opposite direction – where there is a lot of mystery and foggy valleys.

For those with sudden serious health problems, or the many whose dreams for their children can be shattered without warning by an unexpected bomb, we have to help each other live with uncertainty, which, in the final analysis, is perhaps all we really have to share with each other in this uncertain world.

August 25
Hands To Work And
Hearts To God

Walt Whitman (1819–1892) knew first-hand the carnage and destruction of life and dreams during our Civil War between 1861 and 1865. He looked for places of healing and found some on the country's family farms when he wrote, *"A song of farms—a song of the soil of fields."*

These last weeks of August are a time for healing. Sure, laying on the beach can distract us pleasantly, but for deep healing nothing beats being in partnership with nature at this special time of year.

Is there a recommended therapy procedure? Yes, it goes back to Mother Ann Lee (1736–1784), who founded and guided the Shakers. She preached, *"Hands to work. Hearts to God."*

I have found it a rather automatic process. With hands working, our hearts turn to "God" or whatever term a person prefers. And, when my heart contemplates a missing sacred facet in my life, my hands itch to get simple and into the *"soil of the fields."*

There are many different reasons for refreshing our spiritual core on the little patches of earth we each occupy. If you don't live near a farm there is always a backyard, or a park, or a pot on the windowsill overlooking a busy city street. With just a little scratching in the dirt, we can always and in every place find nature's sacred compass.

August 26
Oddball-in-Chief

When I work in the garden I often think of Jesus of Nazareth. He worked with his hands and relaxed with his friends to whom he taught a way of moving through life, of practicing the art of living, which brought hope. He gave himself to all people, including the outcast, the poor, and the suffering. Jesus did not encourage his friends to renounce their humanity but to fulfill it. He rejected religious laws when they stood in the way of human happiness. *"The Sabbath was made for people, not people for the Sabbath,"* he is quoted as saying (Mark 2:27) in a phrase borrowed from the Jewish sage Hillel (110 B.C.-A.D. 910).

Jesus addressed the pains of the people, but he did not fit into any of the acceptable classifications for religious leaders in his day. He was not a priest as were the leaders of the religious establishment, nor was he a revolutionary like the Zealots. Unlike the Essenes, he did not withdraw from society. The Pharisees did not recognize him as a scholar schooled in the intricacies of the moral law.

Jesus was a spiritual oddball who provoked both religious and civil leaders, and eventually he was murdered because of that. To the Roman official, Pontius Pilate, Jesus was a threat to good order, and Pilate eliminated Jesus just as he had many other irritating people. Regrettably we are still doing that.

AUGUST 27
LIFE IS NEW EACH MORNING

Spiritual growth is a continual path. No one will ever reach the end of the road. We are always, in Meister Eckhart's (1260–1328) words, *"beginners among beginners."*

There should be a continual increase of our awareness of everything around us and in us. This means the need to see old things with new eyes. We never outgrow that need.

There are many times in which we slip into a comfortable somnambulant state, or even worse, become an "Old Pro" about spirituality. These can be serious dangers for growth.

Nonetheless, there is always within us the drive toward health and life. Again Meister Eckhart, *"Be willing to be a beginner every single morning."*

August 28
The Gentle Visitor

Coming up to my feet while I was sitting on the porch, walked the first one —an Oregon Snowbird. I had the feeling he may never have seen a human before, but he and his relatives have just flown from their breeding grounds on the Cascade peaks, where probably the first snow has fallen, to their winter quarters on our farm.

They are remarkably frisky little visitors, seemingly finding great delicacies as they scratch the ground. They have several names. The official one is probably "Dark-eyed Junco" but throughout our nation's history they have simply been called "snowbirds." In 1831 John Audubon wrote: "There is not a person in the Union who does not know the little snowbird...so gentle and tame does it become that it forms a companion for every child." And their call is a wonderful overture to the slowly changing season.

Despite the fact that most birds have a violent end to life, they value peaceful and cooperative existence. They cooperate and share, especially with the young whom they protect as best they can. Watching the birds, I experience the shadow of some of the troubles facing humans today. And,

I hope that some relative of my visiting snowbirds can at least "be a companion for every child" who has had to face hardship and loss.

As for me, I don't think it will upset the balance of nature if I just scatter some surplus garden seeds around for our little visitors. And with each toss there will be a prayer.

AUGUST 29
BRING AN EMPTY CUP

There is a Zen tale I like. This is what I remember of the story:

Once Master Nan-in had a visitor, a restless student who wanted spiritual help and he wanted it now! The student's questions flowed without ceasing. Quietly the master offered tea. Even while holding the cup in his palm the student talked on about his concerns and desires. The master poured. The student talked. The tea filled the cup. Still the student talked. Still the master poured. The hot tea overflowed. "Hey," shouted the startled student, nursing his smarting hand, "can't you see this cup is full!" "Just so," said Nan-in, "and, like the cup, you are filled with your own ideas. How do you expect me to give you anything unless you offer me an empty cup?"

In my spiritual quests, I often come with a full cup, or at least half-full.

AUGUST 30
A BREAK AT NOON

I am impressed by the creativity of people who work in 9 to 5 positions and find a way at noon to take a short spiritual break. One thing I have learned from some of them is the advantage of a slow walk. I try to see things I earlier passed by in my hurry to get to whatever task I was performing. There are flowers in the cracks of the sidewalks, and birds do fly in the sky above the trees and buildings.

One of my favorite spots in San Francisco is a park in front of an old church. It is surrounded by trendy restaurants where some of the city's movers and shakers come to maximize the advantages of their business lunch. When I am in one of these eateries, there is a sense of high energy. The relentless drive of my fellow diners is often jarring to me.

I feel more at home across the street in the park. When the Angelus bell rings, the parochial school students go into the church. The bell also seems to be a signal for old men and women from Chinatown to practice Tai Chi and other forms of graceful spiritual movement. College students munch on bagels, which they share with the birds. All manner of people, some with care etched in their faces, take their places on the benches with the same solemnity as if they were sitting down in a church pew.

Actually, I feel that way myself. I look around at this open-air congregation and I feel God's presence among us. This too is a holy communion.

AUGUST 31
A QUIET PRAYER

"Prayer" has many definitions, but I've always found it truly to be a touching, something that teaches me how to reach the quiet within me.

There are many ways to do this, but I've found that one of the best ways is to stay within my inner stillness as if I were waiting at home to quietly welcome a guest and guide. Then I may feel a gentle, soft touch. Sometimes I can reach out to that which is touching me, gently take my guide's hand and be led deep into the waters of solitude. In that place I might have the chance to leave behind all games, all desires, all greed, all dullness, all masks, and loneliness.

That moment of such a touching is an instant of death and new life. Just a moment but... Once again, seeing the same world with a new awareness. Now on with life — one breath at a time.

SEPTEMBER

September 1
The Wheel Turns

September can be such an ambiguous month. I have waited so long to harvest the bounty of the garden. That time is here, but I fear it could soon be over. So many special people touch me, but they are here and gone. It seems like such a short time since all the trees around me were blooming and now the autumn colors begin to appear. I feel like shouting, *"Slow down! I want to enjoy this moment longer!"* But all of life is contained in each moment from our first breath to our last. And the seasons frame those eternal now-moments.

This is a time for storing souvenirs of precious moments in hand and in heart. But also time to move on, without fears or regrets. Tying all that changes together somehow takes our hand and gently guides us forward.

SEPTEMBER 2
STANDING STILL AND
WATCHING TRAVELERS

Every summer swallows come up from South America to where I live in California. They have many tasks to perform: nests to build, eggs to lay and hatch. And then encouraging their offspring to have the courage to fly!

Reflecting on this time of year the Persian poet Rumi (1207–1273) may have had swallows in mind when he wrote, "*Something opens our wings.*" And that "something" produced a faith which allowed the swallows here, big and little, to circle and circle today until they knew that all could make the flight back to the warm plains of Argentina.

There are also those of us today who stand in one place and watch the miracles of our feathered companions. And, as I take my eyes off the sky, now empty of our swallow guests, and look down, I see that snowbirds are still arriving from the already cold mountain peaks of the Northwest.

These little travelers are part of the "something" that opens my soul!

September 3
There Are More Things
In Heaven And Earth…

At this time of year, it seems shadows of people I have known can be found walking in supermarket parking lots. Sitting on park benches. Standing in crowded subway cars. Near a bush. At a table. And always in the halls of hospitals. And also for me there are the old monks who lived centuries ago and who have some vague resemblance to the image I see in the mirror every morning.

Throughout the day, these shadows play hide-and-seek with me wherever I go. We are told we must live in the real world. But what is the REAL world? Do you ever also wonder?

SEPTEMBER 4
THE ATHEIST AS
THEOLOGIAN?

A friend of mine once told me that he was an atheist "by default." He would not accept the false gods created in the likeness of religious fundamentalists and used by them as tools to fashion the peculiar societies they advocated.

The angry old man in the sky who conveniently denounces everything that is opposed by rigid bigots is a false god created by rigid bigots for the convenience of rigid bigots. In refusing to accept these gods, my friend was unknowingly advocating for a more open image of God.

Some contemporary theologians suggest that atheism could sometimes be a criticism of a particular image of God that attempts to put the concept into a box made of doctrines. St. Augustine (354–430) said a long time ago, *"If you are certain that you understand God, it is not God."*

Can my friend be unwittingly calling for a more authentic understanding of "God?" I think he might find that disturbing. I don't.

SEPTEMBER 5
AN INDWELLING GOD

Each one of us can encompass only a part of reality. But the concept of God ought to be something bringing unity and summing up all reality. Impossible? I hope not.

Academics sometimes talk of "Transcendence", which comes from a Latin word for raising oneself beyond ordinary human experience, and "Immanence," whose Latin roots refer to remaining in. Should we look for God above a cloud of incense or squarely in the middle of ordinary human experience?

My own lifelong spiritual quest has turned toward an immanent or indwelling God coexisting

with all of creation. If God is existence itself and each of us is a participant in existence, then God permeates the world and each of us.

Maybe.

September 6
One Leaf At A Time

I can see the first yellow school buses on the county road. Here in California's coastal hills the atmosphere is a bit on the arid side. We are harvesting in the garden and the orchard, and trying our best to keep the greenhouse cool. Like everyone else who looks out at our parched hills we wonder when the rains will come.

Years ago I planted several Sweetgum trees to provide some color to our landscape. They are now very tall. I walk past them several times a day and dearly love them. The tops of the trees are still bright green but the lower limbs have beautiful red and russet leaves. Each tree is becoming a dramatic torch of autumn color. And it is happening one leaf at a time!

You ever have the feeling that God is smiling? Even if you have some questions about "God"? I think this is one of those times.

September 7
Hope For A Suffering
World

As I write this, someone I have long admired is in a coma following a massive stroke. He is on the bridge between life and death. He was a peacekeeper and taught a multitude of people how to be better aware of the suffering around us: of those struggling to survive as the victims of war; of the powerful nations amassing weapons of destruction; of the exploitation of the vulnerable; of our obligation to the beings without a voice who inhabit this earth with us.

He also taught that we must not only focus on the sufferings but also on the fact that a rose bloomed this morning, that a bird was singing with the first dawn light, that a child woke up and smiled, that it was important for all of us to smile.

No matter how frightening the savagery of life, we must not ignore when a rose blooms.

SEPTEMBER 8
THERE WAS A TIME WHEN
WE SHARED WITH EACH
OTHER

I have heard people of all ages expressing disappointment in institutions they would like to rely upon – but cannot. We see disturbing developments in our political structure, educational landscape, religious organizations, etc., etc.

Many "Depression Era" elders, like myself, grew up with the presumption that the common good played some role in our lives. That seems to have become an old-fashioned idea. Now it is the interests of the "significant players" in government, finance, society, church that are to be advanced, or even more simply — what do I get out of this?

Probably, like every other child born in 1931, I can remember carrying a covered dish down the street to some family in "hard times." It seemed natural. Part of our membership in the human community. Jesus said we should feed the hungry — for that matter so did Karl Marx.

SEPTEMBER 9
LISTENING TO THE STARS

Every once in a while where I live at Starcross, we have a Holy Day, or in this case a Holy Night, that you probably will not find in any other community's liturgical calendar — but which is fairly universally observed by individuals all over the world. Coming up is our Festival of the Stars. What's the point?

It has to do with a greater awareness that we are part of something beyond ourselves. Americans place a high value on our individualism, even in matters like prayer and meditation. The Tibetan Buddhist Chögyam Trungpa (1939–1987) termed it "Spiritual Materialism" — it's all about ME! Even when it comes to spiritual growth. As a result, we sometimes feel lonely. That's where the stars come in. Just step outside, which is something human and other beings have been doing for as long as we have walked on this planet.

Well, the process is simple. We go outside and open ourselves to the night sky and be open to what we each experience, or as the earth's First Peoples would have put it — *"Listen to the stars talking to you."*

September 10
Quiet Prayer

As a young child, I prayed by talking to God. Rarely did I simply listen for God. But somehow, like everyone else, I did eventually learn to value moments of stillness. Through the years these have become increasingly necessary for me.

The Persian mystic and poet Rumi (1207–1273) wrote something I find very helpful,

> *"The tongue is the enemy of the soul. When the lips are silent, the heart has a hundred tongues."*

Technological and social revolutions have accelerated the pace of change during my lifetime. Adapting to such rapid transitions has been difficult. Like others, I often feel an imbalance between the life I live and my desire to find a quiet still-point in the midst of events that at times seem out of control.

For me, the balance can often be found in quiet prayer. Prayer that does not ask for anything. Times when I simply sit and listen. St. Benedict (c. 480–547) begins his Rule for Monastics with,

"Listen with the ear of your heart."

That is good advice for everyone.

SEPTEMBER 11
A QUIET MOMENT IN
THE DESERT

Every September 11 our nation stumbles around for a reaction to the brutal attack by 19 members of Al-Qaeda which resulted in the callous loss of over 3,000 lives.

Everyone has stories of where they were on 9/11. Some are dramatic. Mine is not. Flying back from London to San Francisco, our plane was ordered to land in Edmonton. The Canadians were sympathetic, helpful, and not sure what to say. Two days later, the plane was routed back to London. I jumped ship and managed to find a rental car in Edmonton. Driving across the plains of Alberta after harvest time, it seemed as if time were standing still.

When I stopped to eat at a casino outside Winnemucca, Nevada, the first thing I noticed was a lack of noise. CNN was showing images on several TVs but the sound had been switched off. Ranchers were nursing their drinks and thinking — it seemed to me they were absorbing the catastrophic events into the strength of the desert. One by one they paid the bill and drove away.

I remember those ranchers every year. Their quiet pondering makes more sense to me than all the bellicose words I later heard.

September 12
As Autumn Comes

I love autumn. But, for some reason, this year I have
really resisted its coming. Maybe that's part of the aging
process — just trying to get everything to slow down a
little. However, I can no longer be in Autumn-denial! The
trees around me are beginning to dress for their annual
display. And, this week I have been watching a little gray
squirrel diligently searching out and carrying away what
he or she will need for the winter....And so, *"Welcome
Autumn!"*

In not too many days the Autumnal Equinox will be upon
us. The sun will be more or less shining exactly on the
equator and the hours of daylight will more or less be
equal to the hours of nighttime. After that, in the Northern
Hemisphere, the time of darkness will increase until the
Winter Solstice in December. If we let it, there is an opportunity of increased reflection as the natural world around
us does in fact slow down.

Where I live it is the time of the late apple harvest. Also,
the Jewish festival of Rosh Hashanah, the Jewish New Year,
occurs around this time. I am told that at Rosh Hashanah

some folks eat apples dipped in honey, hoping for a sweet season to come. We should all try it, it can't hurt — may we all have a sweet Autumn!

September 13
A Spider and her
Mandala

In the small space between two poles on the railing around the Chapel, I discovered a small and beautiful web shining in the morning light. A tiny spider, no bigger than a pinhead, was busy weaving her silver mandala. She seemed completely confident about what she was doing.

Mandalas have always fascinated me. From Tibetan Buddhist monks, to Navajo sand painters, to medieval rose window designers, these circular constructions have always represented a spiritual universe. I had the feeling this was true of the little spider I watched at work. So many different threads but each one had its place.

I was a bit jealous. In my life there are many things going on and I'm not sure how they all fit together.

September 14
Courageous People in
the Struggle

The supermarket parking lot was crowded. I was leaning on my walker waiting for the others to finish shopping when he came up to me. He was a little younger than me and asked me some questions about the walker. It didn't look like he needed one. I felt there might be something else on his mind. He was carrying a bottle of bourbon. *"My daughter tells me I shouldn't be drinking this. The doctors tell me I have only a month to live."* In the next 15 minutes the conversation got very real. Then we hugged and wished each other well. He walked away into the crowd — with his bottle of bourbon.

Issa (1763–1828) is my favorite haiku poet. He had a hard life and his poetry reflects the struggles of humanity. In his later years, he planted a chestnut tree in a sunny corner of his garden. It seemed to do well. But his neighbor added a new addition to his house which blocked light and rain from the little tree. Also, each winter snow off his neighbor's rooftop fell on the little tree breaking the tree's tiny limbs. But it was a courageous little tree and kept struggling.

Somehow the struggle, for each of us and for society itself, contains within it the meanings and the joys of life.

SEPTEMBER 15
SINGING AND FILLING IN

As we age, we lose things. And we lose people. We should mourn those losses. If we do not mourn we cannot celebrate the new things we find.

My friend Elizabeth Bugental (1926–2009) observed that "mourning" and "morning" go together. Experiencing both the loss and the new wisdom, Liz said, is what makes aging a profound human experience. This is true if you are 7 and learning the full story about Santa Claus, 17 and in the vortex of existence between child and adult, or 70 plus and have asked the question "If I lose, will I be able to go on?" The blank can be filled in with the name of a person or a changed state of being. And perhaps you have even, at least briefly, thought of how to exit this life in a dignified manner—mourning without any hope of a new dawn.

Liz's husband James Bugental (1915 -2008), an eminent psychologist and author, had a stroke which wiped out his past memory. Often at frustrating times for him she had to remind him he had lost his memory. She recounts in her book AgeSong that Jim would then smile and say, *"But I have you."*

We have all worked hard to create lives worth living. So we fill in for each other when we get lost. If I can't remember the name of a person, someone around me supplies it. If I find myself wandering in a monologue, I can ask, *"Is this what we are discussing?"*

It is a compact that keeps life flowing – thankfully.

SEPTEMBER 16
THE GOD EXPERIENCE

There have been many mysteries in the human story. Our prehistoric ancestors used "God" to explain many things that have now become clearer. When I was a child, "God" could fill in a number of blanks in my understanding of life which have gradually been discarded. But something remains. And that something is always changing and shifting as my awareness of life expands and contracts.

There continue to be many struggles about "God." One is between those relying on "revealed truth" and those exploring "an evolution of consciousness." My own present concept of "God" is somehow indwelling and yet co-existing with all of creation.

Where will it all end? I don't know. But I do know that we need the life experiences of all of us, including those who comprehend things differently, to construct some kind of sacred mosaic that will help us find a wholesome and healthy path into the future.

SEPTEMBER 17
WHEN THERE IS NO
DESSERT MENU

I think the most agonizing loss is the dying and death of someone so close and so important we cannot always tell the difference between "me" and "us". I was sitting behind an elderly couple at a concert a few days ago. As the music enveloped all of us, their hands would find each other. Later, it became clear there were blanks in their ability to communicate as they once had. The music helped fill-in the blanks.

Two dear friends, whose names I have changed, had to walk that path. Tom was a brilliant psychologist and a jazz musician. Ruth was in advanced stages of Alzheimer's. He never diagnostically labeled her. Ruth was always just Ruth. When she required specialized care, Tom moved a piano into the care-facility and played there every day. And later Ruth had a heart attack as Tom was playing. She died in his arms.

Earlier when someone suggested Tom should be more "realistic" about the situation he responded sharply, *"Ruth and I have had half a century of a good life together. What do you want me to do now— ask what's for dessert?"*

September 18
Unplug And Be Mindful

Through the digital world we can be connected to so many things that we are overpowered. There is nothing we cannot plug into. We can become so involved with other people's stories that we cannot find our own. So we are reversing the old adage, and today we can't find the tree because of the forest.

But nature can help us turn the tide in our own lives. It can become a spiritual compass leading to a simpler life. In this cusp between summer and autumn, even a short walk can guide us from complexity toward simplicity and peace. How do we start?

Just open the door. Step into a garden, or a city street, a forest path, or a little park. Birds may be singing. Cars may be moving up and down the road. Different stories may be unfolding. There will probably be trees with the leaves falling. And there will always be the sky with its beautiful mysteries.

SEPTEMBER 19
NONE OF THE ABOVE

The Jesuit theologian Karl Rahner (1904–1984) once observed, *"The number one cause of atheism is Christians."*

Recently, the majority of North American young people, when asked to designate their religious affiliation, checked *"none of the above."* This created considerable panic in the headquarters of religious institutions. And it should. Official denominational organizations have had many centuries to get their act together, and they have basically messed it up. As far as those professing to follow the path that Jesus laid out, they too often, as Karl Rahner also once observed, *"profess him with their mouths and deny him with their actions and this is what an unbelieving world finds unbelievable."*

So where does this leave us? Are the coming generations going to be guided by nothing more than self-centered preoccupation? Will concerns for the common good completely vanish? I don't think so.

I recently had the assistance of a very bright twenty-something who considered herself totally free of organized religious influence. When I mentioned that I thought in a particular essay directed to people her age it would be wise for me to stay clear of the subject of beliefs, she strongly objected. *"Working on beliefs is what my generation should be doing!"*

This may be an important time for extracting the very best in the long spiritual heritages that are at our disposal. The process is taking place in the daily lives of ordinary people as they search for the best way to meet the challenges of these times.

September 20
A Good Neighbor

I think my basic Judeo-Christian spiritual heritage is summed up by prophet Micah (6:8), *"This is all that is asked of each of us, to act justly, to love tenderly, and to walk humbly with your God."* I move beyond that only with great caution.

Before the term *"Christian"* was used, *"Followers of the Way of a Jew named Jesus"* was common. Followers or not, all in western society have been influenced by that heritage. For me the essential message of Jesus was compassion — "suffering-with" humanity. It can be exemplified in a story, a parable, he told (Luke 10: 29–37) when he was asked by a lawyer to define *"neighbor."* It is a familiar narrative.

A traveler was attacked, beaten, robbed, and left in bad shape by the roadside. Two professional religious people - a priest and a Levite - happened to be traveling by that same road later in the day. Seeing the injured victim, they refused to get involved and passed by on the other side of the road. Then a Samaritan came that way. Samaritans and Jews were divided by religion and politics. They did not normally associate with each other. Authorities in Jerusalem looked down upon Samaritans with contempt.

When the Samaritan saw the injured man by the side of the road,

'he had compassion on him' and helped him. He bandaged the man's wounds, put him on his own mule, brought him to an inn, arranged for him to be cared for, and paid the cost of his accommodation.

"Which of these three," Jesus asked the lawyer *"do you think was a neighbor to the man who fell into the hands of the robbers?"* The lawyer replied, *"The one who showed him kindness."* Then Jesus said *"Go and do likewise."*

How do we *"Go and do likewise"* today?

September 21
Where Do We Spit?

Hawaii is a beautiful place but not many years ago there was the hell hole leper colony of Kalaupapa on the island of Molokai. That is where a cantankerous priest named Damien (1840-1889) lived and died at the age of 49. He has been made a saint but he fought tooth and nail with church authorities while he was alive. He would bend church rules in order to practice compassion. The issue was often one of inclusiveness. His people, those exiled leaper brothers and sisters, were not to be excluded.

Both the government and the church were very concerned about political and religious agendas, and they did not want Damien to upset the delicate balance. He wanted the lepers to be treated humanely and have places to live and worship. This was still the time when new lepers were sometimes released a mile out to sea. Not all of them made it to shore.

Damien was ordered not to report on the conditions but he gave stories to the foreign press. He followed the way of compassion rather than secular and church authorities.

On visiting the church Damien built with his own hands at Kalaupapa, I was very impressed to find holes in the floor. Lepers often had to spit. That kept them from going to church. When Damien discovered this, he cut holes in the floor. Now they were together in church as a community.

I felt at home in that church — I think Jesus of Nazareth would have as well.

September 22
Harvest Moon

The Autumnal Equinox is one of the four corners of the year. There are significant changes coming!

I watch for the full moon which comes nearest to the equinox. It was once called the "Harvest Moon" as farmers could see well enough to bring in crops in the cool moonlight. Picking tomatoes — or "Love Apples" — in the moonlight was outlawed by the Puritans for fear it would make people overly amorous. Happily, that attitude drifted away.

There is day and there is night. But when that great Harvest Moon is shining there is something else. Like many people my age, I am often awake in the middle of the night. It is exciting to step out into a world familiar to me in daylight yet, so different at night.

In the pale yellow moonlight, the trees are all the same color. Redwoods, firs, fruit trees –blend into a shadowy commonness.

While the moon is full, if I am very lucky, I may see, and hear, the first of the wild geese heading south.

September 23
Everything We Have

Sara was a bright and active ten-year-old. One day she was riding her bicycle home from school, wearing her helmet, when she was struck by a speeding car.

For several days, Sara's father was at her hospital bed as she drifted in and out of consciousness. The doctors were unsure of the future. Dan, Sara's widowed father, was an active craftsman who had trouble accepting that there was nothing he or anyone else could do.

Late one night the nurse checked the tubes feeding Sara, pulled back the curtain dividing the quiet room, and left. After a few minutes Sara slowly opened her eyes. Dan knew that look of confusion but before he could say a word of reassurance Sara's eyes closed. Without thinking Dan stood up and went to the bed. He placed his big hands gently but solidly on Sara's bandaged head. He did not say anything. Whatever strength Dan had was being offered to his child in this ancient ritual of blessing.

In the weeks that followed, Sara improved. Months later, when I asked about her memories of those bad times Sara told me she remembered the time when, *"Dad gave me everything he had."*

SEPTEMBER 24
A MEADOW

My friend Robert Duncan (1919–1988) opened a poem with, *"Often I Am Permitted To Return To A Meadow."* I never really got beyond that line. We each *do* have a meadow where we can return and be completely at home. The older I get the more literal that has become.

All the events of life seem in sharp focus at times. The death of a child. News we did not want to hear from a doctor. Being ill when others are depending on you. Increasing personal issues. Mobility. *"What is the word for... ?"*

But, there is also a life which is bigger than our problems and challenges. There is our life in the meadow. I am learning to occasionally leave everything that weighs on me and step into that meadow. It is not an escape from reality but finding it. Sometimes the meadow is literal and sometimes a part of my story. It doesn't matter.

Surrounding the clearing in my meadow are the trees. Some have been here long before me and almost all will be here when I have finished my journey. At my feet are little wild flowers. Their life cycle will be over in a matter of months. The trees, the flowers, and the people are all one community of creation.

A yellow butterfly is moving over a patch of tall grass. Around me, and in me, are stories of life, death, harmony.

September 25
On Holding A
Grandchild

Holding my three-year-old grandson Damien in my arms I have the unspoken grandparent's lament. I want to go forward with him in life but that will be limited, won't it?

However, Damien will help me remember some of the really important things in life that I have almost forgotten. Someone recently suggested that these included clean pajamas, wet hair, a quiet moment and a "creative" prayer, *Good Night Moon* for the 5000th reading, looking at a sleeping innocent face and then looking out at the moon I have known all my life.

> *On his grown-up face the moon which I have long loved will tenderly shine.*

What can I give Damien? Oh, I have looked ahead a little bit. I have planted enough fir trees to be remembered by him for many a Christmas. But, there has to be more than that. Listening to his peaceful slumber sounds, I can only imagine what the world will be like when he holds his own child. It's exciting to try to look ahead – it is also frightening. The world my grandfather experienced bore very little resemblance to the one in which I have lived. How can I contribute to an environment about which I really know nothing?

I've come to the point of believing that anything I can do to increase the importance of love in my world will improve the environment in which Damien and his children will live. And, if I can't help that process along very much – there are always the Christmas trees!

SEPTEMBER 26
DUCKS SEEKING A
PROPER HOME

The Cistercian-Catholic monk Thomas Merton (1915–1968) described himself as, *"A duck in a chicken coop."* He could have been speaking for many of us who never quite fit in any religious environment.

For me, there was always a little difference. My family cared for my body and mind. The society in which I developed was loving but also judging. As I grew my spirit often had to fend for itself. There was church, but that was not my own experience. My beliefs and religious practices were often extensions of my environment.

Many of us wandered quietly from one soap box to the next, in and out of religious communities, growth centers and psychologists' offices. We, like Merton, were ducks in chicken coops. We could peck away at the food and benefit from various environments but we never really felt at home. Some were able to live in the rarified atmosphere offered by a number of Eastern spiritual teachers. Most of us longed for something more earthy and familiar.

This spiritual home we are seeking must be real. The problems of our lives cannot find rest in a romantic tea house of the imagination. Eventually we probably realize that our first steps to the light are in the murky fog of the fears from which we have been fleeing. And, as Merton put it, *"if we give it time, it will make itself known to us."*

September 27
A Backyard Temple

This time of year I sometimes feel as if I am in a great cathedral as I look at the trees and plants around me. Like many others through the ages, I was taught as a child to dip my fingers in holy water and make the sign of the cross when entering a church. And it seems entirely appropriate to me these days to wet my finger with the morning dew as I walk into this season and attempt to become truly mindful of what is happening around me.

Here where I live, the green sameness of the late summer growing season has changed in just a few days. Overnight our great hickory tree has become a yellow torch. Everywhere colors suddenly appear and change. The shades of green in the orchard are gone. The leaves of the apple trees are waxed and rust, yellow, and vermillion. The pear tree is deep red. Yellow blackberry leaves entwine Redwood stakes piled up against a weathered shed.

There seems to be a unique way of experiencing the sacred in each passing season. An old apple tree is covered in the spring with white blossoms — then fruit — then autumn foliage. Looking at an old tree, I sense something of the cycles of my own existence and I feel at home.

September 28
If One Life Has
Breathed Easier

I have a lot of opportunities for sitting on a bench and watching little creatures at my feet or birds in the sky or any number of things on the horizon. But I don't very often just sit in town and watch people passing by.

A few days ago I found myself trapped, as I at first considered it, in a supermarket parking-lot for half-an-hour waiting for a friend. Resisting the temptation to reach for my iPod or cell phone, I decided to look at the faces of folks passing by. I was shocked to find that not a single happy adult face passed in front of the car window. I'm not exaggerating — every adult seem troubled, or angry, or sad, or fearful.

Does our unhappiness have to do with satisfaction — or rather the lack of it? We all seem to be dissatisfied about something: money, prestige, accomplishment, etc., etc. Maybe at some point we took the wrong fork in the road.

Back in the 19th century, even after the horrors of the Civil War, many people would have agreed with what Ralph Waldo Emerson (1803–1882) suggested should make us satisfied with life: *"... to know even one life has breathed easier because you have lived—this is to have succeeded."*

Well, what did old Emerson know about the challenges of modern life? Perhaps more than we realize.

September 29
A Man, A Tent, A Cat

Weaving unobserved down the city sidewalk and almost invisible among the hurrying after-work crowd was something unusual: an intense young man carrying a tent and a cat.

Probably he was homeless, hence the tent. Probably he was compassionate, hence the cat. It was a very peaceful-looking cat, riding confidently in the man's arms. The cat was at home. He or she knew they were where they belonged.

I can only guess at the stories behind the man with the tent and the cat. But they both seemed to know their place in the universe. In that, it seemed to me, they were unique in the bustling crowd.

And I wondered about myself...

SEPTEMBER 30
THE COMING OF THE
AUTUMN WIND

Late September is wonderful! Its colors and sounds and smells often dictate what we think about. Personally I love growing pumpkins. Their color stands out against the browns of falling leaves around the trees and the grays of fading stalks in the garden. There are also unique spiritual quests associated with this beautiful time of year.

Some poets, especially in Japan, traditionally referred to these inward pursuits as Autumn Wind. Issa (1763–1828) felt this wind as behind him encouraging his feet to return home — to leave the busyness of spring and summer and turn back to the essential core of his being.

The older we get the harder it seems to find that direction. Issa gazed at the night sky and wondered, "Under which star will I find my home?" I think a lot of us can resonate with that feeling.

Autumn is not just about pumpkins and scarecrows, although I love those things, but also these are days that call us to deep awareness of our existence. Again, Issa:

It is no small thing to have been born a human now that Autumn comes!

OCTOBER

OCTOBER 1
PEACE AMONG WILD THINGS

It begins with a few leaves. A couple of weeks back, I looked out my bedroom window at the tall sweetgum tree next to the chapel. It was a column of green going up about 60 feet. A raven was circling the top, and then I saw them — a small cluster of red leaves, harbingers of autumn! By Thanksgiving, this tree will be ablaze with shades of red, warming the heart as the days grow cold.

There had been so much activity in the garden, the barn, and the kitchen, I felt as if summer would go on forever, but after seeing those leaves, I walked around looking at all the other deciduous trees. There was a change everywhere. And with each tree I became more aware of that transformation in the season, the air, and in me.

If we allow it, a quietness can descend upon us at this beautiful time of year. There is a peace to be found if we rest among wild things. For me it always begins with a few red leaves.

OCTOBER 2
QUESTIONS AT SUNSET

As evening draws on in this season, it often seems as if I can relive facets of my whole life as I watch the stars appear. Sometimes that is with joy, remembering the nourishment of relationships or the ongoing unfolding of the sacred in my experience. Sometimes there are personal regrets, or sadness.

I am not fretting about what happens after death. My concern is how I make it between 85 and my last breath. Moving from physical independence to dependence. Pain. Loss of energy. Memory issues. Financial insecurity. The challenges for those close to me, about which there is little I can do. Mostly I think it has to do with my doubt about remaining ME for my children, family, friends — and for myself and my God.

I remember the advice of the old Rabbi to an overly-pious student: "God didn't ask you to be Moses. God asked you to be you!" So to the unknown darkness I pray — "Help me to be me."

OCTOBER 3
STILLNESS TRUMPS
RESTIVENESS

Once I came upon a war veteran working in our olive grove. She told me she was there because she heard olives trees were a symbol of peace. I asked if it helped. She said "yes." This young person knew she had been wounded and was in a process of healing. Often we are all in wars of various kinds. We do not always know we have been wounded and are in need of healing.

We often have too many things hanging on to us, too many desires inside of us. Sometimes the weight of all our possessions and longings will press us down until we are almost too weak to start the day. We have been whizzing around so much that all our inner strength has been used up in gaining, mastering, competing, and possessing.

When we become still and peaceful, the inner strength with which we were born begins to build up again.

October 4
An Instrument Of Peace

Buddhism teaches respect for all "sentient beings." How inclusive is that? One definition of "sentient beings" includes all those who are capable of experiencing suffering. Today is set aside to remember perhaps the most radical Christian ever, Francis of Assisi (1181–1226) who also looked on all creatures as brothers and sisters.

There is a legend of Francis and the wolf of Gubbio. A lone wolf was terrorizing the town. Francis approached "Brother Wolf" with respect and made peace between him and the townspeople. They would respect and shelter him. In turn, he would protect them. The wolf's anger abated and he placed his paw in Francis' hand. Was this literally true? It doesn't matter.

When we are looking to our own sense of community, how is "we" defined? What about people who are a different color, culture, citizenship? How can we all be part of an extended family? If I can feel at home with a fruit tree and a bird, and maybe even a wolf, why not with every human living on earth? Yes, it is harder. But in truth, we are one people. Let there be peace.

October 5
From Green To Yellow
To Brown

One October morning I discover our great hickory tree has become a yellow torch. Unnoticed for months, the tree now commands attention every day. When the leaves turn a rich brown, they begin to fall, making their way through the branches and onto the ground where the slightest breeze helps them hop along. As the hard nuts fall from high up, they strike the branches and produce a windchime which seems to encourage the response of the many birds resting there.

Everywhere on the land, colors suddenly appear and change. The shades of green in the orchard are gone. The leaves of the apple trees are waxed in rust, yellow, and vermillion. The Bosc pear tree is deep red. Yellow blackberry leaves crawl over the piles of redwood stakes piled against the weathered shed. And, I will never tire of spotting the orange pumpkins emerging from the foliage of the vines.

At some point, and not for any particular reason, I move from tree to tree collecting a basket of colorful leaves. It is a slow process during which I sense something of the cycles of my life. I feel a kinship, and I feel at home.

OCTOBER 6
A GENTLE BREEZE

In the American southwest, I heard a Kachina carver speak of being guided by the sounds coming through the canyons and the rock formations. Another time, I listened with reverence to a soldier speaking of a celestial hum in the night air after a devastating battle. When Buddhist monks chant "OM," I wonder if they are not imitating that hum. And, I have no doubt that it all helps to heal the world.

At home, I often hear the wind-chime that hangs outside the chapel — part of autumn's music. A little farther away is the sound of the wind in the trees. And, on some still, late afternoons I can hear the throb of the ocean several miles away. Native peoples say we have forgotten how to hear the hum of the stars but on some nights I think we remember — a bit.

Today is a good time to listen, to be healed, and to heal.

October 7
When Every Family Had
A Fruit Tree

O n a warm October day, I was sitting in our orchard with a friend who had come up from Los Angeles. It was a special trip. He was frail, partly blind, and would die in four months. We both knew that.

It was late in the afternoon. The fading light filtered through the few red, yellow, and brown leaves that remained on the fruit trees. Our conversation turned to things my friend could still eat and enjoy. He mentioned apples with some longing in his voice. I got up and walked to a nearby tree that still had some fruit. He was amazed when I put a large yellow apple before him. There was a long silence as he stared at the apple. Then he spoke of the homes of his boyhood in New England.

"I had forgotten," he mused, "there was a time when every family had a fruit tree. To eat the fruit of a tree sharing the land with you makes a difference in how you live your own life." It does.

October 8
What Has Been And What Is To Come

On the first wind of autumn comes the final fragrance of summer. All the apples have been canned or frozen, the keepers have been stored. Today every apple that can still be found on the trees has been brought to the barn for cidering. Often these are the sweetest from high in the trees where they were overlooked in the frenzy of earlier harvests. I enjoy collecting these. It is a slow process with plenty of time to reflect on what has been and what is to come. Even the pressing seems a contemplative process.

Soon the scent of the pressing travels beyond the barn. This cider will be enjoyed in the months to come. But today the aroma is to me what incense is to the monk in the temple. So many things in life are like that. I have a friend who is a very successful attorney and parent and who gets the same meditative experience from slowly washing and drying dishes. There are so many paths to the transcendent in life; apples, incense, dishwater...

OCTOBER 9
USING THE NIGHT SKY

Most of us, perhaps in the dim past, have gone outside under an autumn night sky to help a child become more aware of the mystery of life. I remember one time when the starlight was so bright that it made silhouettes of the tall trees surrounding us. I said what I had to say and then followed a long silence. I knew something was happening but I had no words to describe the process then or now. The closest I can come is to say that there was a communication between the stars and the child. I've heard of First Peoples who facilitate this encounter. For example, a mother raises up her baby and asks that he or she receive the heart of a star — a celestial baptism.

Searching for words and images, we come up with phrases like; "the indwelling spirit", "the divine spark residing in every person", "the hand of God." The mother holding up her baby doesn't need words. We in the "civilized word" are more comfortable when we put a verbal frame on an experience. But the night sky can never be contained in a box of words. Yet there is something there that can be used when times are dark and confusing. Used, but never completely understood rationally.

October 10
Treasures Of The Day

O ften little beings connect us to the real world. My infant grandson Damien and my cat Tigger know nothing about the "important" things that occupy my day and mind. However, they can occasionally lead me to a simpler place— if I let them. At those times they are important anchors to keep me from drifting into turbulent waters.

At night, as I look back on the events of the day, I sometimes ask myself which of those things I have experienced would I have wanted to do if it had been the last day of my life. So what do I treasure? Watching Damien lock eyes with his mother. Sitting beside Tigger just after sunset and gazing out into nothing —or was it everything?

OCTOBER 11
A FAMILIAR SONG

On these October days, I sense that somewhere there blows a soft wind that carries a silent song I would find healing. Often my mind is filled with questions, arguments, and expectations. If I give up the inner noise, the silent song may enter in.

The breeze that bears the song may come from the deep stillness that surrounds our universe. It is perhaps its nature to enter into any silence it encounters.

Once, an elderly Shaker told me to learn from the willow tree — it only has to stand still and the wind moves its branches.

Maybe the wind and the song have to be understood as something we always have — a stillness at our core. What we came from and to which we will return.

OCTOBER 12
FAITH IN STARDUST

"Faith" is a difficult term. There are very few references to it in the Hebrew Bible. In contrast, Paul's letters in the New Testament allude to the concept two hundred times! To many Christians, "faith" quickly came to mean revealed truth that has to be accepted, and church leaders are to decide what is an authentic revelation. I don't think there is much future there.

But "faith" can also mean confidence. I trust, for example, that God is with us in the life we share with each other. Others are more comfortable expressing the same concept in a different way. The vocabulary does not matter. Many, if not most of us, have confidence that we are each able to encounter a transcendent reality. No one person has the whole truth about this spiritual process.

As I stumble around with the ordinary tasks of life, I often sense that I have one foot in the realm of the spiritual. At times, I worry about words. At other times, I don't. On some of these beautiful October nights, as I look at the sky, it fills me with awe to realize that the earth was formed from the dust of exploding stars and that each of us is composed of atoms from the stars. Stardust is my essential being. At these moments, my faith simply means respecting my stardust.

October 13
Looking Through
The Broken Window

Some days are hard to take. Anyone who has suffered a loss knows that. And some heavy days just seem to go on-and-on. One of my perennial sources of inspiration has been the spiritual sojourn of the lay-monk and haiku poet Kobayashi Issa (1763–1828). Throughout his troubled life, Issa was searching for beauty.

During the weeks I was receiving daily treatment at a cancer clinic, I recited one of Issa's poems often on going out the door. The haiku contains only a few words in the original Japanese: "loveliness," "rip/shoji screen," "milky way." I read it this way:

How lovely it is
to look through the broken window
and discover the Milky Way.

It is not easy to look beyond the broken window of a shattering loss and experience the wholeness of the Milky Way. But we can. Issa hungered for beauty, peace, and harmony. But he, like all of us, had to find those graces while sometimes surrounded by sickness and decay.

OCTOBER 14
A FESTIVAL OF LEAVES

There are many holidays in autumn. However, my favorite is one you will not find on any calendar. Our family has an annual "Festival of Leaves." Without using that title, I know that millions of people are doing the same thing. In backyards, parks, farms, and forests, trees changing colors are the highlights of the season. In Northern California driving home, I see the yellow maples and remember the red maples and oaks, the aspens, birches, alders of the New England countryside. Around the last curve, the red and yellow torches of our sweetgum trees frame the chapel. Next to the barn the fruit orchard offers its multicolored crescendo.

If you are my age, there is a place to sit and contemplate whether the leaf drifting slowly to the ground has any poetic or spiritual significance. The younger group just jumps along kicking the browning leaves. On one day, we each gather those leaves —every one of them telling a different story about the tree, the past, and the future. Then we put them all together for a beautiful display.

So what's the point? Don't let the moment pass! Go where the leaves are to be found; watch the autumn wind play with them.

OCTOBER 15
TRANSENDENT WHEELING

The line between a blessing and a curse is sometimes very bendable. Because of a nerve problem, I was strongly advised not to walk. Being in a wheelchair is not my image of myself. I remember a line from a book I read, "Then they wheeled in some old guy who I had never heard of." I don't want to be that guy! But despite great resistance, I ended up wedded to a wheelchair. What a curse. Or, was it?

I discovered some surprising advantages to the wheelchair. I did not realize how much I had been racing around. Now, as I slowly propel myself down a familiar hall, I am astounded at all the things going on in the garden outside the windows. There were many other examples of this "handicap." Instead of racing into the chapel, there are very beneficial times on the chapel deck discovering views I never knew were there and hearing the songs of birds that are new and refreshing to me.

Because I was stuck out on a porch waiting for others to bring some tea, I saw a little fox looking for water. Somehow the line between human and animal became very thin. In fact, the wall between me and everything else, including God, become more transparent those days in the wheelchair.

OCTOBER 16
BUILDING FOR ALL

Recently I attended a memorial gathering where a large extended family was coming together after a young person's death. There were people of every age, and I realized how important it is to understand that each one of us lives between the generations who have gone before us and those yet to come.

We each really do make a difference. And, therein lies our hope. Take a moment and think back. In each of our stories we find so many people who were there for us at the needed moment. Probably we didn't realize it; just as we likely don't realize how our own sufferings and joys build for all.

But they do.

October 17
A New Day

Before I have been up an hour, I can already cross several items off my mental "things-to-do" list. Even a morning prayer can become simply a task to be performed, so much meditation, so many psalms and prayers. This is really not very satisfying.

When I have nothing to do but become aware of the new day, then I can be open to spiritual nourishment. I live in the country and can walk among trees as the dawn light comes through the branches and wakes up the world around me. When the leaf changes color or the bird sings, I feel my soul being refreshed. But a person does not have to have beautiful trees and pure air. I have watched the dawn light coming through the haze of a polluted sky in an Eastern European city hard hit by an unsuccessful revolution. Never did I feel a greater sense of hope and renewal.

In the early morning, I like a time of quiet meditation in a sacred place. For me now, this is usually a little chapel, but it has also been under a tree, in a train, or in the bathroom with the noisy sound of children beyond the door. It doesn't matter where. What I call God rides in on the dawn light.

October 18
How Is My Neighbor Doing?

Years ago, when I was traveling through rural Vermont, I noticed that every small farm had some little display emphasizing both the season and something unique about the family who put it together. Inspired, we started putting something on the road in front of Starcross – his name is Chester. He sits on a hay bale and cheerfully greets passersby with a *"Hi there"* gesture. Neighbors often wave back.

As he was experiencing the challenges of a final illness, the poet Basho (1644–1694) wrote,

> *Deep autumn*
> *my neighbor –*
> *how is he doing?*

It seems to me that people who have accepted that they are on the final journey often have great wisdom and can express it in simple and profound ways. I hear Basho saying that he no longer has to worry about tomorrow – at such a moment, we can genuinely escape from ourselves and ask, *"How is my neighbor doing?"*

OCTOBER 19
A QUIET TIME

As the day moves on, I look forward to Vespers, or as the Anglican Community terms it "Evensong." It is a wonderful time in a small spiritual community like ours. The day's work is over. Light is fading. After a day of crossing tasks off a list, it is sweet to regain a broader perspective by singing and meditating together.

But there are times when I am away or caring for someone. What works best for me at those times is to take a few minutes before dinner. I find a calm place, choose a psalm at random, read it, and spend a few moments in quiet reflection. It is an arbitrary ritual. I think anything would do. The point is to remember we have a spiritual rhythm in our lives. It is important for us we take a moment and break the chain of activities. A time to remind ourselves there is more to our lives than things to accomplish. A time to be refreshed by the silence, and perhaps the song of a bird bedding down.

Prayer? Connecting with the sacred? It happens by itself. If we give ourselves some space. Some quiet.

A friend of mine begins her short spiritual break in the evening with the simple question, "In the last days of my life, what will I recall from this day?" It is a good question.

October 20
When There Is Only
The Breeze

I live close to the land, like our ancient ancestors, and the seasons of the year solicit a spiritual response. Frosty spider webs, apple blossoms, the song of a meadowlark, the sound of water, wind in the trees, the sight of the morning star are all wonders that lead me to an awareness of the sacred and help me understand my place in the changing rhythms of history.

But I have a friend who lives far from a farm, surrounded by the concrete towers of a major city. Her little room is high in one of those towers. Old, nearly blind, and experiencing pain when moving, she nonetheless opens a window every morning, feels the breeze and listens to the sounds which travel to her on the air.

Both my friend and I want to allow the seasons to prompt us to live in harmony with nature's cycles. Generally, she is more successful at it than I am. Perhaps she has fewer abstract issues to put aside. Something for all of us to remember as the years roll by.

OCTOBER 21
SPACE FOR PRAYER

Work has a way of filling up our lives. This was especially true of rural people in former times. Various reformers attempted to enrich that existence. One was St. Benedict (480–547) who strove for prayer and work, "Ora et Labora", in his sixth century rule for monks. That sounds pretty dismal to 21st century ears, unless we remember in Benedict's Italy normal farm life was all "Labora" and all day! Benedict was calling for something beyond the work grind in daily life. The concept of leisure was not anything to be considered in the struggle for survival which preoccupied most people of his time. But life should not be all work

How do we make time to turn our hearts to God? This was the motivation for the well-ordered communal life of Benedict's monks, to make space in life for contemplation. The key is to make spaces in the work schedule. Once that happens another phenomenon can be encouraged, which is seeing the sacredness in the work itself. In time, the difference between "Ora" and "Labora" may fade. Then, as the early Shakers taught, "Every breath is a continual prayer to God."

OCTOBER 22
THE BITTERSWEET LIFE

After many decades on a meandering spiritual journey, I have a growing satisfaction with simply living my life in the confidence that God is with me and with us all. Many of my struggles with anxiety and fear have been related to a false assumption that my life should be without shocks and troubles. My life is bittersweet, and that is as it should be.

There were times in my life when numbers mattered. How many people can I help? How many spiritual roads to peace can I explore? Now, the whole of God, of humanity, of the cosmos, of my life, can be in the experience of one child, one person — one moment.

OCTOBER 23
WHEN THE DAY
BRINGS PEACE

As the years go by, wholeness, peace of soul, and spiritual comfort now come to me mainly in the ordinary moments of daily life. My experience of God comes in a gentle breeze. The places where I have truly opened myself to the divine presence have been next to a sick child, planting a flower, watching a bird, sitting on a train, washing clothes, listening to children making music, cleaning a small chapel.

That is the sort of hope I want to leave those who come after me, especially those I love: the understanding that looking at a sunset can change your life, smelling the air on a autumn morning can make you aware of God, being with someone who is dying can splash you with the peace that heaven wraps around those who are leaving us, touching the hand of someone who cares can make us deeply understand the "Good News" of any spiritual tradition.

October 24
What Matters Most?

I was born in the Great Depression. There were scary times. The owner of the house we rented burned it down for the insurance. He thought we were not in it. We were. The core values of my life came out of that bleak era. I have been thinking back on how my parents survived. There were a lot of issues I grew up with — including food. "Soup" was my mother's response to any monetary shortfall. But there were also spiritual survival tools.

My parents chose one thing they would not lose. For a young child it was like a game which became a mantra. We will lose a lot of things but we will be OK so long as we have "family", a sense of warm connectedness. We lost the house and furniture, presents at Christmas once, movies often, free-time to afterschool jobs. Whenever there was something I planned on that had to be discarded, my mother would pull me out of gloominess with the reminder that we were alright as long as we had family.

Now, in these senior years of losing various things like mobility and vitality, what is the one thing I will not lose? It remains a good question.

October 25
Bad Times And Good Neighbors

A monk who had been imprisoned in China once sang a song in our chapel. He had composed it in captivity. The first line translated something like *"God never promised that the sky would be always blue."* It is important to know that applies to all of us. Perhaps it is our most important common ground. We learn it from our parents. We teach it to our children.

A memory drifts in of when I was a young child. Times were bad. We lived down the street from a widow with children. We didn't get along with her very well but she was the hardest hit in our neighborhood. I would be handed a hot dish wrapped in a flour-sack towel. My instructions were very clear! I was to put the dish on her porch, knock, and walk away. I was NOT to feel righteous. The widow was NOT to feel humiliated. Poverty was no disgrace. I learned that we gave and the widow accepted because we felt our common ground. It was the right thing to do.

We must combat that soul-sucking feeling of facing bad times alone. We should look for neighbors in material or emotional need and push right in with a helping hand. It helps them but it helps us even more.

May our people never forget this.

October 26
An Old Tree And An Old Man

Sometimes old age can be a bit overwhelming. I was recently considering various troubles when I looked at a large, ancient, huggable, fir tree. OK old Tree, what words of wisdom do you have?

"Don't fret over the lack of the best environment or lament over the absence of the finest nutrients. Just use what is at hand. Live the simple life. Never lose your awe of nature, of what is around you. Put down roots. Only then will you awaken to the strength within you."

Are you happy Tree?

"I am me and I am growing where I was planted. I will die but I have been part of the community of life."

Well, what does a tree know? None-the-less a hug would feel good.

OCTOBER 27
HOPE IN THE MOONLIGHT

Those in the Islamic tradition speak of *taqwa*, a consciousness of God, as the central theme of the month of Ramadan. In the Oakland hills, that process of a heightened sense of the divine begins as Muslim children focus all their attention on the moon. At first they see nothing in the sky; then the thin crescent of the moon appears. Any quest for the sacred is often that way. First comes only a brief glimpse of what we hope for. Is it real or not? Slowly our hope, like the moon, waxes.

It is good for all of us to occasionally go back to those days when most people marked time by watching the phases of the moon. All any one religion can do is present a facet of divine beauty that can never be fully comprehended by any single individual or faith community. The moon, or the sound of a distant bell, or a candle flame can remind us that there are times when we must each travel undistracted. Life can sometimes be a serious challenge when we need a consciousness of the sacred. It usually begins with a thin sliver.

For some children in Oakland, it may also involve eating dates in the moonlight.

OCTOBER 28
REPAIR THE WORLD
WITH MUSIC

Tikkun Olam, or "repair the world," is one of the obligations of everyone living in a Jewish tradition. It is a directive we should all embrace. The world never has been and never will be without need of repair. It is like an old beloved automobile. Something always needs to be fixed. And, each of us is responsible for maintaining some kind of fix-it shop in our lives.

Anytime the clash of words and ideologies fills the air, as in political disputes, or when there is a great soul-sucking pain or tragedy that cripples a family, community, or culture, we are in need of a transcendent healing. Music can provide part of the repair the world regularly needs. I expressed this idea to a violinist close to my heart. He looked up at me and said simply, "That's why I do it." Probably every musician understands that they are needed to regularly repair the world, although they would express it in different ways.

We do not always have a musician but we always have the winds of autumn. Much too gentle to be a threat, they are not only felt but heard. Different sounds come from different trees as they move in the wind. God conducts a full orchestra!

OCTOBER 29
AUTUMN HANDS

A poet I knew many years ago wrote of the wind blowing leaves across his autumn hands. I think that's what I am experiencing now. I want this earthly paradise of red and golden leaves to continue forever. I want time to stand still. But it doesn't, does it?

It is the suddenness that I object to. I am not ready for someone I love to die. I am not ready to stumble along a path where once I ran. I am not ready to witness things I loved destroyed. I am not ready to so frequently lose the train of my thought and my sense of direction.

"Be honest now," shouts the wild wind, "would you ever be ready?" No, that's right. This is not the scene I would have chosen but it is part of my life —part of God's gift to each of us. So let us open ourselves to whatever blows across our autumn hands.

Are you are too young for autumn hands? Then follow my cat's example. Curl up before the fire until this all blows over. Because, for you, it will. And, probably for those of us with autumn hands as well.

OCTOBER 30
WHEN THE RAINS COME

When I was young, Hermann Hesse (1877–1962) was my favorite author. Some things he wrote I only now understand in old age, such as:

> *You are not the master of yourself, you are a bird in the storm. Let it storm! Let it drive you!*

In nature, as in life, scenes can change rapidly. Today at dawn it seemed as if we would have another endless and beautiful day of autumn but clouds appeared in midmorning. The sky darkened, and at noon, the first raindrops appeared. A flock of snowbirds headed for protection in the branches of our olive trees, quite a different haven from their summer shelters in the tall firs and pines of Oregon's Cascade Mountains.

The winds of autumn are mostly tantalizing. They cause the cornstalks and the tall wild oats to gracefully wave. They ruffle our hair gently to help us be more aware of the remarkable beauty around us. But sometimes winds become storms. And that is what happened today. By mid-afternoon the rain was being thrown hard against the windows. I thought of the snowbirds and hoped they were safe. Actually, that is also my hope for myself. And, I ponder Hesse's challenge to the birds and to each of us: *Let it storm! Let it drive you!*

OCTOBER 31
SEEDS AND PIES

At this time of year, and in the late afternoon light, my favorite corner of our garden is a spot where I can stand facing a patch of pumpkins while listening to the rustling of dried corn stalks behind me.

Those who work in the vineyards of Northern California sometimes say when they taste a wine they have helped produce they can experience again the whole year of growing, harvest, pressing. That would be a bit over-the-top for my pumpkins, but I do remember the seeds in my hands. The little green plants. The first blossoms. The swelling orange globes. And, I can really taste all that when the finely seasoned soup appears, and the curry, the ravioli, —and yes also the flans and the pies!

Tonight, some strangely costumed seeds of the future generation will appear at our door and ask for treats. All too soon they will become too old for this. And, I will miss them, as I will all the blazing leaves of October.

November

November 1
Autumn Prayer

Often prayer is not something we set out to do, but something we can't help doing.

In the past half-century, there has been a slow realization that prayer, encountering the sacred, like any other kind of experience or learning, can be found on different paths. Most of us started out with words and reflections. Many moved on to silence, meditation, emptiness. But the autumn of the year calls for us to use even more elementary intelligences in prayer.

Walking in a woods or park or even in the backyard, we feel the same rush of awe as when we step into a great cathedral. The color of the leaves and also the starkness of the branches, take us out of ourselves – thereby removing a great obstacle to becoming aware, "mindful" as Buddhists would put it, of the creative pulse of life. As we take the last tomato from the garden, or clip the last rose, we know we are not alone but in partnership with some other part of creation.

For me, autumn is one of those times when praying is simply being here.

November 2
A Time For Remembrance

H ave you ever noticed that there is a kind of melancholy which often descends as autumn fades? It is as if we are ignoring something important.

It was 1999, I was 68. My parents had been dead for some years. The AIDS pandemic had taken over my life and losing friends became a common occurrence. It was *All Souls Day*, November 2nd. I went to hear a quartet in Berkeley, the free-thinking-secular-capital of the universe. In that concert I was introduced to the rich Mexican tradition of "*Dias de los Muertos*," the Days of the Dead, which combines all the best elements of *Hallowee*n (October 31), *All Saints Day (November 1)* and *All Souls Day (November 2)* with a vital and nourishing human dimension.

Días de los Muertos resembles festivals in many cultures where people come back to the family home, clean the cemetery where their relatives are buried, and celebrate being family together. Home altars are constructed on which those we love are remembered in various ways. In my present home, we set up a table where we place pictures and memorials of people, now gone, who were — and are

— special to us. It is comforting for me to recognize that in some fashion we are together again.

Death is not separate from life. They go together. Looking at an altar of remembrance I hear echoes of people I knew and loved. Most relationships bound by love will never completely pass away.

November 3
The Barn

For me, the barn is a second chapel. There are times when its mammoth interior is filled with noise and frantic activity. Most of the time, however, there is a deep quiet leading to memories. I have wandered in this structure, transplanting memories from other barns. I remember the smiles and laughter of little ones, now almost grown, working and playing. I recall the solace of finding an excuse to be alone in the barn after the loss of a child. There have been many gatherings, dinners, parties here. The soul of the farm, and maybe of the farmer, is in the barn.

I want to simply be an elderly worker in the barn, taking time to gaze out the big door at the trees in their autumn colors and the arriving birds from the north. But in the distance I also hear the voice of children, some close and some very far away. As we get older, it is good to be around understanding younger people, as I am blessed to be.

Most people don't have a barn. But there is always a window, a porch and chair, a tree, or a flower pot.

November 4
The Old Oak

We came to our farm in 1976. The first thing that greeted us was a giant live oak. It is a good three stories tall and has been standing here through all kinds of weather and social changes for a long time — a beloved symbol of peaceful stability. In the summer, we have often gathered to pray, or simply reflect, where the oak looms like a massive religious sculpture at the end of a row of olive trees.

Now we have been told the tree can no longer sustain life, and that one or more of its massive limbs is likely to fall in the winter winds and injure humans or animals. The responsible and prudent thing to do is to begin the difficult task of cutting down this great tree.

It is important to take anything concerning the end of life seriously. This is a sad task to perform. But before we start I want to remember: the flocks of birds that nestled in its top, the mistletoe the children gathered each year from its lower limbs, the heroic stance it took against gigantic winter winds, the shade it produced in summer, the mountain lion that slept on a branch for a few days each year, the mating heron couples that would gather at the base, and the many people who leaned against the trunk and privately confided in it before walking on into life.

For me the quiet strength of this tree has been a reminder of what a monk, or any person, should be.

NOVEMBER 5
A BLESSED TIME

November can be a healing time. In Northern California, where I live now, there is often no real rain until late October. That first rain seems to draw a curtain across the stage of my anxieties and preoccupations. The scene has changed and the damp earth softens the pace and the shrillness of my life.

My steps no longer echo on the parched and hard ground. They are cushioned and I am aware of new sounds. The gravel paths have a deep crunch which I both hear and feel. A little snap is added as I step onto the carpet of twigs and cones under the pine trees which surround the house. Standing beneath the branches of those pines and looking out on the horizon, I feel both engaged and protected. There is a divine presence in there. And, also in me.

November 6
Green Tomatoes

From time to time our garden has a Year of Green Tomatoes. We did everything right; heirloom seeds, fine little plants in the greenhouse, transplanted to the garden, tended with TLC. But a weird and cool summer —and no red tomatoes when the first frost comes.

At every stage of life, we can have Green Tomato problems. Don't make it into the right pre- school and the rest of your life will collapse like a row of dominos! Ok, suppose you do all the right things and graduate from the right college with the right degree. There is a recession. Your dreams collapse. Green Tomatoes. It just keeps going on throughout life.

My thoughts jump to Viktor Frankl (1905–1997) who began his healing career with Viennese university students who failed in some way and felt their life was over. Suicide was rampant. His efforts helped to turn that around, and in time led him into general issues of the vacuums which sometimes consume us with emptiness, boredom, apathy. Then it became personal when Frankl was a slave laborer in a Nazi concentration camp, and they burned all his writings. In that hell, he experienced the essential need to always find meaning in life, and a reason to continue living no matter what the circumstances.

I wish the tomato I hold in my hand was not green. But it can remind me that it is possible to look beyond the frustrations, disappointments, and even sufferings that will inevitably come my way.

November 7
Thinking in the Rain

Come February, I really get tired of the rain. But now, in autumn, I love how it freshens up the earth. A gentle rain leaves an aroma, a sort of thanksgiving incense. Of course, all winter rain is not welcome. Fierce storms can bring downpours and do great harm.

Buddhist monks who live in lands with definite rainy seasons learn to use the time for a long annual retreat where they study and reflect upon life. There are many rain haiku poems. The Japanese poet Buson (1716–1783) created an image of a child's cloth ball on the roof being soaked in the rain.

As the rain falls on the roof
a child's forgotten rag ball
is drenched out of shape.

For me, the whole manufactured world is in that ball decomposing in the rain. Perhaps the dreams of childhood are also fading up there.

But all is not dour. The Spanish mystic Teresa of Avila (1515–1582) wrote of watering the garden of spiritual growth. Some days we must laboriously haul water from the river; at other times we may be able to use a well and an irrigation system. However, on some days it simply rains. Ah, if it be so let it rain today!

November 8
A Little Patch Of Earth

It is good to regularly become mindful of the ground at our feet and the life around us. Why? Nature can always be a spiritual compass for us, no matter how bad the times we face. All that exists is ever in flux. Becoming really attentive to the changes in nature helps us to understand that we are part of a bigger process.

Sure, our life can be scary and out of control. One of Jesus' most common sayings was, *"Be not afraid."* In many stories about Siddhartha we find the person who ferries us across the river saying the same thing. Are you old enough to remember the TV show *Star Trek*? Once we are truly aware of the place where we dwell and the changes in the seasons then, as was often repeated in the show, we may find it easier to "boldly go where no one has gone before!"

I value a slow, walking meditation where I move in rhythm with my breathing. The important thing for us to understand is that we are where we belong and that we are supported. Maybe you are not able to walk around at the moment. I have been like that. Then, I look out the window. A few times, there has been no window but I have memories.

So, in good times and in bad, let us become aware of the little patch of earth on which we live, and — *"Be not afraid. Go boldly where no one has gone before!"*

November 9
Take A Hand And Make
Holy The Day

A famous Lutheran scholar, Rudolf Otto (1869–1937), attempted the difficult task of defining "holy." He said it had three elements. It was mysterious, terrifying, fascinating.

How do I make this day holy? There are many different answers. However, I have faith that if we become aware of the mysterious, terrifying, fascinating, transcendent experiences going on around us, the wisdom will be given each of us to open ourselves to the sacred dimensions of these days.

A friend, in very challenging circumstances, responded to my inquiry about how things were going by saying, *"We're at the stage where the most important thing is just to hold hands."* In one way or another, that is what will make this day holy for many of us —holding hands when it matters.

November 10
A World Beyond

A redwood and Douglas fir forest surrounds my home on three sides. On the open side are vineyards. I am mostly aware of the sounds of birds and other little creatures among the quiet thoughts and movements of peaceful human friends. However, I am mindful that this place is an eye in the storm of contemporary life. When everything is still, I can sometimes hear the world of machines beyond the trees. At night there is often the lonely hum of a car mixing with the call of an owl or the howl of a coyote. In each of those sounds is a story of life to which we are all connected.

No matter where we dwell, each of us is in the eye of a storm. The morning paper or the evening news can reveal the tempest surrounding us which is also a part of us. In these November days, as the trees drop their leaves, the far sounds seem to come closer and mix with the crunch of autumn leaves under my feet.

The connection with the world beyond can also work in reverse. Sitting in the sterile and foreign surroundings of a hospital waiting room I can hear, with my ears or my heart, the wind in the tall branches of the distant forest trees, and I understand that world is real, and I am a part of it. Despite the anxiety, the panic, the emergencies which surround me, I know that what is written in ancient texts like Isaiah 14:7 is true:

The whole earth is at rest, and it is calm...

November 11
Poppies

We now call today "Veterans Day". In England it is "Remembrance Day" and everyone wears a poppy because of a poem Dr. John McCrae (1872–1918) wrote:

In Flanders fields the poppies blow
Between the crosses, row on row,
That mark our place; and in the sky
The larks, still bravely singing fly
Scarce heard amid the guns below.

Hopefully we are all remembering the day an armistice ended World War I – a bloody, stupid and pointless conflagration in which 20 million people, almost half of them civilians, perished for something called "National Honor."

I never was in combat. In my college we were required to serve in the Reserve Officers Training Corp. I was Air Force, and scheduled to go into the Korean Conflict (officials didn't like to call it a "war.") But I was found medically unfit. This was the forgotten war that took the lives of my friends and classmates. At a funeral, someone whispered to me, *"Old men make wars that young men and women die in."*

War may sometimes be necessary, but our involvement must be more than simply watching reports on the evening news. It begins with remembering. As long as we have sent people into the fields of battle, the very least we can do is to remember the poppies in Flanders Field.

November 12
Transcendent

I am one of those people who feel that to be complete my life has to include something of the sacred — the holy. "What the hell do you mean by that?" asked a frustrated friend. A fair but difficult question. People have tried to answer in many ways with words, poetry, music. The best answer I can come up with for my friend's question is something like the Buddhist concept that I have to get outside myself in order to be myself.

The environment often helps me get away from my preoccupations and open to the transcendent — the holy — the sacred. Music is a frequent aid. Visiting beautiful churches used to help. But in our rapidly shifting religious landscape I no longer feel at home in most of those places and besides, at night they are locked. Like other older people, I shuffle around at night and usually all I have to do is step outside to enter a great cathedral that is truly mysterious, terrifying, and fascinating. On a clear and cold winter night my experience often centers around the beauty and grace of the moon. Simply stepping into the moonlight is usually a way of resetting the necessary balance and harmony of my life. Is this an experience that only a rustic and aging monk could come up with? No.

Whatever our questions, there is no better place to be than under a wintry night sky. At least in that one place and moment there is more harmony and peace in the world. All we have to do is open the door....

November 13
Stones

One year, my friends gave me a birthday gift of a large boulder which had become dislodged and was blocking a country road. Not such an odd present, for they knew I feel there is something sacred in stones. Ancient people piled them in mounds to mark holy meeting places. Their descendants learned to fashion them into temples. Other people's descendants sometimes tore the structures down in an attempt to destroy the soul of a people.

Romans destroyed Jerusalem's great temple in 70 CE following a Jewish revolt. The only thing left is the Western Wall. It is a retaining wall that supports a hill known as the Temple Mount, which is sacred to Muslims, Jews, and Christians. The wall is constructed of magnificent stones from many time periods. It was said to be near the western wall of the Temple's Holy of Holies, from which the Divine Presence has never departed, according to some Jewish traditions. It is easy to believe that. I was there on a day when Palestinian militants up on the Mount were fighting Israeli militants down below. Yet along the wall there was peace.

What was I doing while leaning on those stones? Just being there and feeling the presence of God, of history, of my own life. I have the same feeling coming upon a moss-covered rock in the woods. It is good to touch it and let our stories merge.

November 14
A Common Journey

When I started taking daily radiation treatments for cancer I was fortunate to have a very competent and considerate medical team. But there you are in your short gown trying to keep some degree of modesty while at the mercy of people young enough to be your grandchildren!

Once the self-consciousness fades and I am waiting for my turn under the big machine, I realize anew I am sitting with others who are sharing this unasked-for journey with me. Some are afraid. Some are frail. There are common concerns: pain, money, energy, decline. In short, here I am in a group where each of us is wondering if our warranty on life is running out!

So why isn't everyone sad and depressed? Most of the talk is about the future. Some here may not be part of it, but there will be a future. Trees will grow and so will children. Somehow each of us have been, and will be, a factor in what happens in the future.

There is a Maori proverb I learned: *Turn your face to the sun and the shadows fall behind you.* Every day, I came out of the cancer clinic unburdened by trivial matters and with much more awareness of family, birds, flowers, and the lives of people I had just met. Now I no longer need the radiation, but I still need to be aware of what really matters — every day, every minute.

NOVEMBER 15
HARVESTING TOGETHER

Watching rain clouds cross the pale moon, I think of the Native Peoples who once walked this land. The November moon was the warning sign for the time when the water would freeze and life would become hard. The challenge of this month is that we not stand alone in those hard times.

We appreciate the support of strangers extending a helping hand, not because they know us, or like us, or because of what we have done, but simply because we exist together on this planet.

At dawn, I watch the heavy morning mist rising from the rivers until only the tops of the evergreens are seen. The few leaves on the trees are bright ornaments. The earth, here in California, is dark green. Our olive trees are laden with fruit, green and silver leaves shimmer in the breeze. In mid-month we start the harvest and begin pressing the oil, a centuries old process requiring many hands. Friends and hired helpers from different places, cultures, and generations are harvesting together. Neighbors we seldom see during the year take up their specialized places in the pressing process. With all these contributions, a lovely oil is produced to be enjoyed all year. It takes a group of people to make that oil. Each year I think that this solidarity is needed in any important human venture. We really have to help each other.

November 16
Guided By Doubt

Before we were born we never wondered who we were. There was peace in our mother's warm womb and no need for hope. The sounds and light of life were filtered through the skin of the other human in whom we had begun to live.

But all things change and anxiety replaced security as we began our journey into the world. Ever since that moment we have felt a little out of place. We are each on a quiet pilgrimage in search of a home.

In this lifelong quest, uncertainty can be a holy guide.

November 17
At The Crossroad

Individual spiritual paths continually converge and cross for varying lengths of time. We are all enriched by this progression. Sitting at the crossroad, this is part of what I see:

An Episcopal Archdeacon moving to a Quaker faith, a Baptist divinity professor becoming Dean of an Episcopal Cathedral, a Christian moving to Buddhist to Atheist to Jewish, a secular humanist to Catholic, a Catholic to Buddhist to secular social activist to independent Christian.

My life has been enriched by people on many paths. I cannot think of anyone at this moment who was shallow about the quest.

We are a people searching for the sacred. My concern has been to salvage some of the rich heritage of Western spiritual life for those who can be nourished by it, whatever their background, attitude about organized religion, or beliefs. In some way we all grow by each other's experience.

NOVEMBER 18
LOOKING DOWN

I remember a story in which a student asked the Rabbi, "Why is it so hard to find the face of God?" And the Rabbi responded, "Because you don't look down."

Every day we juggle hundreds of tasks. It is difficult. Where do we find help? Take a pill? Take a drink? Or as Basho (1644–1694) wrote: *"Clouds come from time to time to give us rest from gazing at the moon."*

But today is a cloudless, sunny day so I'm going outside, choosing a square foot of earth and watching it for a long time. I think it's especially good to do this when I become anxious about what I cannot do. After a while, I will rest and gaze around upon all that surrounds this patch of earth that is my home. Will you join me?

NOVEMBER 19
THE CHAPEL

Where I live, we have a little chapel. It has always been a special place where we can go and remember that God is with us, no matter how we may individually define "God" at the time. For me, all of our land is sacred space, but the chapel is one of those "thin places" where the ordinary and the transcendent merge. We simply have to be quiet and let it happen.

The chapel has six sides, with windows facing in every direction. We gather there every morning to greet the day and every evening to end it. When we share the breaking of bread we feel our connection with all who have gone before us. We often share this simple but sacred space with friends. It is a peaceful crossroad at both joyful and difficult times – a place to feel at home.

Over the years, as we have quietly listened in the chapel to God and to ourselves, we have found the path we should follow, and the strength to continue. Many times I have stood on the chapel porch and looked out over our land and the rolling hills beyond, thinking of our place in the universe.

You probably have a little chapel, in your house, outside, nearby. It may not look like ours but it is just as sacred.

November 20
Closing and Opening

Closing down or opening up often depends on whether we have a timely experience of new life coming. It could be an apple blossom or news of a new child on the way.

This year I had three friends die in the same week. It brought back emotional echoes of the worst times in the AIDS pandemic. The person telling me of one death ended our telephone conversation with the words, "It's over." Even in my shock and sadness, I knew there was something wrong with what he said. Nonetheless it is hard not to close down at times like these. We have all had those experiences. But my life, or your life, is not just about me or you.

Many years ago, when I was so young that friends dying was only an abstraction, I wrote: *"You are running in a relay. This is the moment you have been chosen to hold the torch. You cannot refuse to run. Whatever you do is part of your page in the story of life."* Now I know I should have added one more sentence — *"The day will come when you pass the torch, but the story continues."*

One of my favorite Shaker sayings is: *"Open the windows and the doors and receive whomsoever is sent."* For every ending, there is a new beginning.

November 21
Open The Door

Henry David Thoreau (1817–1862) wrote: "*Silently we unlatch the door, letting the drift fall in and step abroad to face the cutting air.*" When I open my door in Northern California, it is leaves that fall in, not snow, as was the case in Thoreau's Massachusetts. Leaves of every color; golden brown from the apple trees, bright red from the pistachio, yellow and orange from the sweetgum, bronze from the oak. But then, like Thoreau, I "step abroad to face the cutting air."

I often imagine other people are doing the same thing all around the planet but especially in the northern hemisphere where the air can be cutting at this time of year. Whatever the destination— city, park, forest, ocean cliffs—there will be sights and sounds that are part of the sacred nuance of the season. Dogs barking. Cars moving down the road. Emergency lights flashing. Lighting the fires. Feeding the cows. Watching the birds. Stories are unfolding everywhere we look. Everything and everyone I encounter is my companion on this journey, including the fallen tree blocking my path, the drug-addict blocking the sidewalk, the distracted attendant at the toll booth. All companions.

Walking along a very familiar route at home between the olive trees and the forest, I become each time more mindful of the bond between myself and the decaying stump, and the bird standing upon it. To the West on a clear day I can glimpse a bit of the mighty ocean. The hills are dusted with frost to the east. And there is always the horizon.

It mesmerizes me. Somehow all the stages of my growth these many years and the reality of where I am today, and tomorrow, meet out there where the sky meets the land.

On a November day, even a short walk can be a holy pilgrimage.

NOVEMBER 22
THANKSGIVING

Fourth Thursday (between November 22–28)

In a few days, Thanksgiving will be upon us. This is our one truly denomination-free opportunity for a national spiritual holiday. In our very fractured nation, this is a moment when we can really come together.

Just a little history — Thanksgiving actually isn't about Pilgrims, Native Americans, turkeys and cranberries. It goes back to the dawn of history. It was present in ancient Egypt, in the Jewish festival of Sukkoth, in the harvest festivals all over the world. True, there was a great celebration at Plymouth in 1621. But it was sort of a one-on affair. Popping up around the colonies were harvest festivals rooted in the many traditions of the multicultural foundation of the United States. Politically it was an up-and-down situation. George Washington proclaimed a couple of Thanksgivings, Thomas Jefferson condemned the practice. Sarah Josepha Hale spent years trying to get a single day on which we would all give thanks. As a result of her efforts, Abraham Lincoln proclaimed a national holiday.

The words of Ralph Waldo Emerson (1803–1882) hope-fully fit in everyone's Thanksgiving:

For health and food, for love and friends,
For everything Thy goodness sends,
 ... we thank Thee.

November 23
Just Before Dawn

As I age, life seems to swing between emotional opposites every day. A stanza from Chapter 58 of *THE TAO* jumps out:

On misery perches happiness.
Beneath happiness crouches misery.

On a good night, my soul may drift happily downstream in sleep. But often, just before I wake there is an anxiety attack which alerts me to the day. There is often wisdom in a morning dream, daydream, meditation which sharpen my life-skills as I encounter the paradoxes of daily living.

Once during the night, I forgot that a friend had died. Then came the oppressing remembrance. Then the sound of a bird on my window ledge. Was the bird "real", or a dream, or a memory — does it matter?

Each dawn brings the promise of brilliance. But there will be shadows. We will have to walk with uncertainty through whatever the day brings. The courage to do this comes from something deep within us, which surfaces with the morning light.

NOVEMBER 24
A SPECIAL TIME TOGETHER

As the denominational and organizational aspects of religion show increasing signs of stress, the need for the home to become a primary spiritual center is correspondingly important.

We can learn much from the traditions which developed during the Diaspora when the Jewish people were scattered from their homeland. The weekly Shabbat meal and ceremonies can be a model for all.

It often starts with a blessing of the children for, just before he died, the patriarch Jacob blessed his children, that they might in turn be a blessing to the people.

It would be nourishing for any family, on any path or none, to gather around the dining table once a week with practices to make explicit the relationship between family life and each one's spiritual life.

November 25
Touching The Ageless

The world is rapidly changing around us. Our comfort-
ableness with institutions, civil and religious, is fading. In personal and family life, we are having to confront
unexpected issues. At times like these, it is well to reach for
something that is unchanging — a renewed taste of the transcendent. And we can find it sometimes in a field at midday.

In late November at our farm we harvest olives, an ancient
practice requiring many hands. Looking down a row of
trees, I see a number of friends quietly working. Each
of them has a story, as do we all. Nearest me is a well-
known professional man suffering from an advanced
brain tumor. Farther down the row is a young veteran just
returned from a war he had begun to question, his mind
now often filled with overpowering images of death and
destruction. Next I see two people silently working side-
by-side. One has spent his life trying to save the futures
of a few of those caught up in the American penal system.
Working on the same tree is a young teenager with serious
social problems. They have never met before. Further still
is a woman who has spent her whole life trying to make
the words of the gospel come alive in compassionate faith

communities. It has recently been made clear to her by an uber-conservative church leader half- her-age that she is no longer welcome.

On such a day, our olive groves are healing fields. There is something growing near everyone that can help transcend our troubles and heal us.

November 26
Welcome All

When I was a child, Sunday Mass was the center of my family's spiritual week. I had no doubt that God was there. As an adolescent, I was excited to learn that God was equally present in the people themselves who had gathered for the Mass. As my spiritual experience increased, I became aware that God was present in many human encounters, which were not limited to ritual gatherings. Any meal can be a sacred communion.

When he walked among us, Jesus presided over meals with diverse folks, many of whom were not invited to the tables of people who considered themselves respectable. He redefined "family" and became the host at the family table. In the process, he restored the communication between the rejected ones and God. Throughout his ministry, Jesus called everyone to a peaceful fellowship when he broke bread. Sometimes it was with throngs in the open air, and at other times it was in small intimate gatherings.

Any meal can become a divine experience never to be forgotten. But today we have the responsibility for inviting the whole family to the table. When we do, we often touch some ultimate authenticity in the unfolding adventure of living.

November 27
At Last There is Peace

Since the wine culture took hold, a valley near me can be quite a circus at times. Land speculators are selling vineyards, and an aristocratic lifestyle, to wealthy buyers. Grand motor coaches, limousines, and luxury cars park beside dusty Fords with Midwestern license plates. People on wine tours come from everywhere, Australia to Alabama, and crisscross the main road with cameras and souvenir wine glasses.

But by late November the grapes have long been stripped from gnarled grey vines. Work crews, machinery, and the hectic pace of the harvest are usually gone. The autumn rains have cut down on visitors. The only buses on the road are those taking children to and from school. Driving through the valley at this time of year, I often see solitary farmers walking down the rows of vines now emptied of their grapes. A remnant of yellow, brown, and crimson leaves hangs loosely on the vines, at the foot of the blue hills

In the fading light of a winter day there is only quiet in the vineyards, a quiet leading us to the sacred.

November 28
Bird Lessons

When I am focused on some difficulty in my life, or in the weather, I often can look out the window and see a bird with a different perspective on the existence we are sharing at the moment. It is not only that she can fly and I cannot. We have common basic needs, which I approach in complicated ways and she with simplicity. She eats, finds shelter, breeds in a natural way. And when she dies, which I am told will probably be in a violent fashion, she will exhibit the same grace. The end is not something that concerns her. It does me. Life is what the bird sings about and what I want to more fully appreciate—up to my last breath.

Gratitude for life enters in here somewhere. That is what, according to legend, Francis of Assisi (1182–1226) was explaining to the birds one day. He and his brothers had been walking along when Francis saw a great multitude of birds. Telling his companions to rest, he went over and preached to the birds. His main point was that they should be aware of the sin of ingratitude. (I wonder whether any complaining brothers were also listening!) Francis reminded his little winged sisters and brothers that, although they did not "toil nor spin," they had clothing, water, food, and all they needed for a happy life. Therefore, at all times and in every place, they should sing God's praise. The birds, and I suspect the brothers, seemed to understand.

These days in late November are good times to look for visiting birds in our backyards or in the trees that line our streets. They are there, and these little creatures bring with them grace, and hope, and sometimes a song—if we will take the time to listen.

November 29
Our Songs

There is a rhythm in all of life, which can only be heard in moments of quiet. If we are in harmony with this rhythm, there can be a sense of unexpected completeness in us and possibly in all the people we touch.

At first, we look outside ourselves for the rhythm, and we only hear a faint sound. Then we listen inside.

When we hear the song we must decide what we will do. We can wander in search of other tunes. We can stand rigid and continue to listen. Or we can let the song possess us and open ourselves to ultimate frontiers of existence.

November 30
A Cloud In Deep Space

The constellation Orion is an awesome sight I have always associated with this time of year. It is on the celestial equator and visible throughout the world. For us in the northern hemisphere it is most striking in the winter months between November and February. In the ancient Middle East this constellation was often related to those mysterious "blessed messengers" who enter our lives from time to time to guide us on our way.

Orion's stars are exceptionally bright and clear. Three in the center are frequently referred to as "the belt." Hanging below the belt is a nebula — a cloud in deep space with the makings of things to come. In all our lives there is also a spiritual nebula of things yet to be. Perhaps in the days to come, this Advent, we can find the courage to become more mindful of that sacred space within each of us.

DECEMBER

December 1
A Time Of Rememberance

Since 1987 the first day of December has been designated WORLD AIDS DAY, commemorating the pandemic that has been so much a part of our lives throughout the world and here at my

home. It is a reflective day at Starcross as we recall the many we have known and loved. They helped us be mindful of what is important in life. That ties in to the gradual spiritual awareness that seems to come upon me, and probably most others, during this month. We all owe a tremendous amount to those who have gone before us and who left us the heritage which we can claim in this month. It is not a time of beliefs and dogmas. It is a time for experience.

In Romania when I worked on opening a home for AIDS orphans, I met a 4-year-old boy named Tenase. He was dying and could no longer eat anything solid, but whenever a treat was being passed out he insisted on getting his. Tenase would then carefully divide the cookie into equal parts and give one share to each child in his room. By his actions he was communicating, *"We have a future."*

I don't pretend to know how it works, but if each of us strives to always remain human, somehow the crooked roads will become straighter.

December 2
A Light In The Darkness

"Advent" means "coming." It begins near the first of December and traditionally is a time of joyful expectation celebrating both the event of Jesus' birth and the building of God's kingdom on earth in our own age.

The season reflects the interrelation between the natural world and the spiritual. The major

symbol of Advent is light. It is a powerful time for me when our little spiritual community gathers in the darkened chapel and we light the first candle on the Advent wreath. Similar things are happening all over world. Lighting a candle is such a natural activity for everyone. It is said The Buddha once taught, *"Thousands of candles can be lighted from a single candle, and the life of the candle will not be shortened."* His point? *Happiness never decreases by being shared.*

Life can be hard. Like everyone else I have been wounded in the process of living. These pains often come to the surface in the darkness of a December afternoon. When the first candle on the chapel wreath is lit, the light helps push back the darkness and the pain.

The challenge of Advent is simply to bring more light and comfort to the world.

December 3
Listening To The Songs
Of December

As I grow older I become more mindful that winter festivals are framed by nature, not religious doctrine. It is in our environment that we can hear the songs we have inherited from our spiritual traditions. This is the month when I try in earnest to hear something of those songs in nature, music, gatherings, poetry and all things that can take me to a place of quiet and simplicity.

We each have special places where it seems the pieces of life's puzzle fit together. The trees. A view. A gravesite. A gazebo. A garden. A chapel. Between where I write and my little greenhouse hangs a wind chime on a bare crabapple tree. There is a gentle breeze blowing. I am going to walk out to the tree and listen to the chimes—my pilgrimage-of-choice.

December 4
God As Stillpoint

My quest for the divine frequently starts with a storm in my life. "God" is the name I often give to the calm eye of the storm. In Asian spirituality there are many references to potters and a "stillpoint."

If a potter attempts to fashion a vessel while the clay is on the side of the wheel, there is nothing but chaos. The force of the wheel works against the process. If the clay is on the center, the potter need apply no force. She simply positions her hands and the vessel is formed. The power of the wheel is now working with her. The presence of this stillpoint allows the spinning sides of the vessel to be in harmony with the force of the wheel and the hands of the potter. All is well.

So somehow what I am seeking is not so much doing as not-doing — surrendering to the moment. A willingness to be led to that stillpoint I call God.

December 5
Anne Frank And
St. Nicholas

At a very difficult moment in her life Anne Frank (1929–1945) wrote this:

> *Let's not forget it's St. Nicholas Eve,*
> *Though we've nothing left to give away.*
> *We'll have to find something else to do:*
> *So everyone please look in your shoe!*

Anne was Jewish but St. Nicholas Eve is not about belief find pleasure in each other. It is not a time of spending but of sensitivity and creativity. Anne was not ready to give up simply because she was hiding from the Gestapo with her family and their colleagues! Is it any wonder she is the most beloved teenager of my generation?

So today what do we have to give each other without adding to our growing December *Things To Do* list? How about *TIME?* Let us take a break from getting things done and simply give each other the gift of time on this St. Nicholas Eve.

Sitting by the fire as the wind blows outside there is sometimes no difference for me between this now-moment and all the other times which have so deeply enriched my life. In this space, those I loved are with me again. Thank you Anne — and St. Nicholas.

December 6
What Grows In Winter?

A great many winter holidays have become increasingly troublesome. We are left with an almost indefinable longing which cannot be satisfied with the trivial, glitzy, forced joviality and commercialism, which surrounds our festivals. Can there be another approach?

Perhaps we could begin with the bare trees around us, and the gray skies, and the coldness. Nature is slowing down. Can I prioritize the need to step off the bullet train of contemporary life?

Our experiences in these days are like small seeds-- we know they are planted within us. But we don't know much more than that. If we give them space, they will grow.

DECEMBER 7
PLAIN AND SIMPLE

My Quaker friend Emily related how her Grandmother Lucy, when encountering a person in stress, would say, *"Friend, perhaps Thee has too many cumbrances."* Emily found this a very good thing to remember when setting her priorities at Christmas time. Her family almost always had a tree. They would sing carols in the evening. Give simple homemade presents to each other. But expensive gifts were not purchased. Cards were not sent out. Rooms were not decorated with the latest bauble. Elaborate sweets were not prepared. The time she saved from not doing those things was used, as she put it, *"in giving and receiving from others, and opening myself to the Light."* Her top priority was to make more time to be with family and friends.

We could all lose the "ought to do" mentality. These December days are full of potential— outside of our window, in the faces circling the table, on everything great and small that we encounter in heaven and on earth!

December 8
Bodhi Day

About six hundred years before the birth of Jesus, Siddhartha sat down beneath a fig tree and resolved not to get up until his mind became clear about the nature of existence. December 8 is the day when many Buddhists celebrate Siddhartha's moment of enlightenment, or Bodhi, under that fig tree.

Siddhartha understood that we all suffer because of craving what we want and running from what we fear. Bodhi Day seems like a good time to focus on the priorities in our lives and to be more mindful of our actions and non-actions. What we learn about ourselves may often be hard to accept, but usually it is valuable to us.

DECEMBER 9
RAIN IN THE CITY

Winter rain is not always welcome to a person living in the country. But sometimes I like being in a city when rain falls heavily on the streets —I don't have to maintain the drains!

For me, rain in a city is like a looping poem in which familiar things are transformed. The dust of past days is washed away. Shoes may be soggy, but they are clean. The wetness creates a community of people with clean, wet shoes. Riding on the T, Boston's subway system, one early December morning, college students had their heads in different books; both the wetness of their hair and clothes revealed a commonness between us. It was the same with younger kids dripping in the aisle and the old man trying to maneuver his umbrella through the door. On some days, it is an easy jump from being soaked together in the subway car to recognizing the divine spark in each of us.

Coming up to street level, next to the exit, I saw a pine tree with a drop of rain on every needle. Sidewalks became mirrors where all the city's lights were reflected. Everything and everyone glistened. I was in a world of shining people!

When we try to maintain planned schedules or become obsessive about destinations and tasks, rain magnifies the absurdity of our efforts. When it is raining very hard, sitting in the shelter of a coffee shop watching the rain is a pretty good non-activity. There is an awareness of the storm and an appreciation for not being in it. Sometimes it is good to stop, to discard those not-so- important-all-so-important agendas. Can sipping espresso in a coffee shop be compared to writing a haiku poem or meditating at a monastic retreat? I think so. The important thing is to acknowledge the rain and to reexamine our priorities. Hopefully, at such moments a kid in rubber boots will come along outside, splashing from puddle to puddle!

December 10
Chanukah Stories

At a certain point in the winter darkness each year, lights are lit to commemorate an ancient miracle. In 165 BCE, a Jewish army drove out an oppressor and reclaimed the Temple in Jerusalem. They cleaned it and removed all foreign symbols. When the time came to light the perpetual flame, as part of the rededication to divine worship, they found only enough oil to last one day. With faith, they lit the lamp anyway, and it burned for eight days—until new oil became available.

In modern times, tiny candles on menorahs flicker in windows and giant gas flames shoot up from eight pipes in the city squares each winter. These lights remind us to rededicate the sacred space within each of us.

Most Chanukah stories celebrate our misfortunes as well as our good fortune. They teach me to appreciate finding a little light in the murky labyrinth of my own life. And that is good enough to encourage me to keep going. Looking through the windows into Chanukah stories, we see: two blind children in a poor house, a dying child, the home of a struggling and oppressed family in Poland, parents

coping with cold and hunger in harsh times, children surviving the Nazis in the Warsaw Ghetto, Auschwitz, a para-
keet on a freezing window ledge in Brooklyn who proved
to be a matchmaker with a taste for potato pancakes.

No Chanukah story has ever left me feeling that my winter celebrations were not going to measure up. Just like
the original event of reclaiming the Temple and keeping
the light burning, Chanukah stories focus on the ongoing process of personal rededication to whatever a person
holds sacred.

December 11
As The Music Comes

When I find cat prints in the hard frost I know my world is changing. "Advent" means a time of coming. But what is coming? All my ancestors have looked for a light in the darkening winter. And the birth of Jesus is involved in that quest someplace. The barren landscape encourages me to make my way to that stable in which I long to find the source of my faith—my trust.

But to do so I must part with my fellow Christians. I suspect it is often the same with friends in Buddhist, Hindu, Jewish, or Islamic traditions. There are always those who announce the wrath of God, from John the Baptist to today's televangelists. It is hard for me to comprehend Jesus as a theologian, or even a preacher. For me Jesus was—is—a song that came upon human history. That is not an original idea and has nothing to do with beliefs and institutions.

T.S. Eliot (1888–1965) reminded us, *"You are the music while the music lasts."*

This is the month when I try in earnest to hear and reflect something of that music in nature, song, performance, gatherings, poetry, and all things that can take me to a place of quiet and simplicity.

DECEMBER 12
A YOUNG WOMAN OF HOPE

Here, at the midpoint of Advent, is a powerful festival of hope — The Lady of Guadalupe.

Twelve years after the Europeans conquered what is now Mexico and attempted to destroy the native culture, a dark-skinned young woman dressed in a peasant cloak appeared to Juan Diego (1474–1548), a poor indigenous worker. Shortly thereafter she presented him with some roses blooming out of season. He gathered them in his rough blanket. Later, when Juan showed them to the aristocratic Spanish church officials, it was discovered that the image of the young woman was imprinted on the blanket. Thus, it would seem, heaven attempted to remind the Spanish conquerors that there was a spark of divinity within each native person they were oppressing. Later, the Lady of Guadalupe became the symbol of freedom in the revolutions against Spanish control.

At a church in my county, slightly after midnight on December 12th, a thousand or more people gather with candles and pictures of the Lady of Guadalupe. They walk singing for nine miles until, about four hours later, they arrive at another church for a fiesta.

I asked a young Chicana teenager why she was so fond of this Lady of Guadalupe. Without hesitation she responded, *"Because she looks like me!"* Juan Diego probably had the same thought.

DECEMBER 13
WHITE CLAD IN CANDLE LIGHT

Today is the feast day of St. Lucy (283?-304?) — Santa Lucia. It is a big deal in snowbound Scandinavia. Girls clad in white appear. The strange thing is that this most famous saint in the far North had never seen snow. She had in fact never been off the Mediterranean island of Sicily. Yet she became a symbol of hope for those struggling to survive the rugged dangers of a Scandinavian winter.

Who was Lucy? No one knows for sure but the traditional tale runs something like this. There was a wave of persecutions against those living the Way of Jesus in her hometown of Syracuse. An angry rejected suitor reported her to the Roman authorities, who sentenced her to be removed to a brothel and forced into prostitution. Then, as the legend goes, when they came to take her she was immovable. Next, she was condemned to death by fire but the flames did not hurt her. Finally, the Romans managed to kill her by piercing her neck with a sword. Somehow, by resisting the suitor and the Roman authorities, Lucy planted a seed which was harvested centuries later in Scandinavia by people needing encouragement.

Darkness can be depressing, even frightening. Under the older Julian calendar, December 13 was the shortest and darkest day of the year. For those living near the Arctic Circle, there is almost no daylight on that day and all kinds of unpleasant fantasies may abound. This might explain why a person in Sweden would be relieved to start the day by having a young girl with long golden hair, dressed in white with a wreath of seven candles on her head, pop into the bedroom to serve rolls and coffee. That's a sure way to dispel the shadows of nature and of mind!

There is a Swedish Santa Lucia song for hope in bad times. It goes,

> *Night goes with silent steps round house and cottage.*
> *O'er earth that sun forgot, dark shadows linger.*
> *Then on our threshold stands, white clad in candlelight*
> *Santa Lucia, Santa Lucia.*

DECEMBER 14
HARBINGERS OF JOY
AND GRACE

Birds, birds, birds. Thin streaks of color against a grey-white winter landscape. Flying from unknown places and using our fountain as a watering hole, a diverse community of December visitors gathers on the stone basin. Some will linger here until the snow melts at their principal home. Others are on their way to some warmer place. This is the mating place for some. They will leave in the spring with the next generation. And, there are those who share this land with us year-round; quail, bluebirds, finches, ravens.

It is the newcomers who especially catch my eye. Flocks of yellow-breasted dancers. Red throated singers. The masked and stately coexist with the shy and tiny. Occasionally, just for a second, a line of cedar waxwings appears and disappears so fast I wonder if I really saw the birds. If I happen to look up at the right time, I may see a lone eagle, or hawk, taking in the scene below.

To my mother, the crimson cardinal was the symbol of Christmas. A speck of red in the bare winter landscape of her youth. Just before she lost her sight, she crafted me a needle-point of a cardinal as a Christmas gift. I have never seen this bird at my California home. But if I should, I would be tempted to believe it was bringing the spirit of the one who taught me to be mindful of the sacred nourishment available at this time of year.

December 15
Many Windows, Many Trees

Tucked between two glamorous and expensive San Francisco neighborhoods are a few streets with aging Victorian houses. I would not describe them as quiet streets because they are home to many children. When school lets out, there is a riot of diversity in ethnicity and dress. But there is also a unity among the kids, which reflects the streets themselves.

Most of the flats have bay windows and this time of year there are lights in almost every window. Though some of the trees bearing lights are evergreen Christmas trees, some are dwarf fig trees, known to Buddhists as "Bodhi trees." The trees may differ, but the strings of lights decorating them all come from the same local hardware store and reflect what we all hold in common. Both the evergreen trees and the fig trees are symbols of the longings of the people who live behind those windows. The trees make the rooms special – and also the streets!

How much can we authentically share in a culture that differs from the one in which our parents raised us? Let's think about these San Francisco school kids. Who are their ancestors? Is the Dalai Lama as real to those students whose grandparents came from Tibet as the American human rights leaders they spoke of in class today? Young people usually work it all out somehow.

Someone told me that the lights strung on a Bodhi tree are always multicolored to demonstrate that there are many paths to spiritual liberation - enlightenment.

In *To Kill a Mockingbird,* Harper Lee (1926-) wrote, *"I think there's just one kind of folks. Folks."* That is what I am looking at — the December windows of folks in San Francisco.

DECEMBER 16
AN OCCASIONAL GRACE

December is a "thin place," to use a term from ancient Celtic peoples. They had in mind specific places, islands or mountaintops, where parallel worlds came together — the human and the divine. But there are days which assault the walls around us, and they can become very thin. This month is one of those times when the sacred sometimes flows into the ordinary moments of life.

Recently two of us found ourselves unexpectedly alone gazing at the fire one evening. Something had gone amiss, and a planned gathering derailed as people had to be at other places. And, there was sickness. It had been a hectic few days with times of both joy and sadness. Now we hardly knew what to do in this unanticipated quiet space. We remembered an old bottle of Armagnac someone had given us years ago. In the glow of the fire, and the brandy, carols came forth like mantras. Even the thin walls faded away. It was an hour in which we felt no separation from the sacred, the ages, or those we loved who were in other places. And, that is how we all, no matter what our spiritual paths, can live from time to time.

Outside the wind is blowing. The stars are bright. A cat is moving toward the door to be let in. Somewhere, in all that, God is smiling.

December 17
The Great O Antiphons!

I spent my adolescent years in a school run by Benedictine monks. By tradition, and in nature, there is a sea-change today as we pass mid-December and move toward the winter solstice, and Christmas. In the monasteries, this is marked by the beginning of the O Antiphons used in the singing at Vespers — the evening choir service. For about 3 weeks, monks have been singing pious little pieces to accompany the psalms. Today, the monks burst out with mantras providing a drumbeat encouraging us to stop protecting ourselves emotionally and to become aware of our deepest inner needs.

The fundamental assumption of the Christmas story as well as that of Bodhi Day, Chanukah and other winter spiritual guideposts is that the divine and the human can touch. It doesn't have to be grandiose. We mustn't be distracted by churches, brocaded vestments, gold chalices, clouds of incense, and sometimes flawed leadership.

Moses found holy ground at the burning bush. Jesus was born in a barn. The Quran was revealed in a cave. Siddhartha was enlightened under a tree. A sacred touching of heaven and earth can continue from wondrous events down through the centuries and into a moment between two old friends in a coffee shop, a family singing around the hearth, a homeless man looking into the trusting eyes of his dog, a woman on her sick bed holding our hand, the Hopi Butterfly Maiden sitting near a mountain of corn deep in the earth, anyone finding God in the rain dripping from eaves outside her or his little room, a monk in a chapel.

Today we can make time to ask ourselves "what is my spiritual hunger?" And in those quiet moments become mindful of the sacred potential in the days to come.

December 18
Swing A Bat With Joseph!

There are going to be difficult winter days. What many of us suffer at some time is the painful attempt to emotionally survive on the margins of the jubilant Christmas crowds. So many personal realities do not fit into the myth of holiday cheer. This time of year there are many reasons for empty places at the table — estrangement, aging, illness, loss.

St. Joseph may be the patron saint of the imperfect Christmas. Poor Joseph. He was engaged to the young Mary. A Jewish betrothal in his day was a powerful thing, and it brought joy to this village carpenter. Then, as Matthew's gospel puts it, *"... before they came to live together she was found with child."* Whoa! All dreams and hearts are broken. But Joseph loves Mary and takes her to his home anyway, and the road gets worse from there. It's no place for the child to be born, having to flee into a foreign land and all the rest of the familiar story.

Some of Joseph's stress is reenacted today in the Las Posadas days held among people of Latin descent. For nine days before Christmas, the drama of looking for lodging, *posada*, is acted out. On the last day the time comes to break the piñata. Each child swinging the bat is blindfolded, but eventually the satisfying crack of the piñata resounds and small treasures come raining down. We can learn from that. Even though we may not always be sure of what we are doing, it is healthy to swing our bat, hoping to crack open something that brings us delight!

DECEMBER 19
FIRST AND LAST

A well-known composition was on the program of a major symphony orchestra, one the orchestra had performed many times. An interviewer asked the conductor how he could find a fresh approach to such a familiar work. *"I always think"* he said, *"that for a few in the audience, this will be the first time they hear it. And for a few others, this will be the last time. This means we have a very serious obligation to do it well."* I think he set a good example for how we should approach many things in life, including the festivals of winter, no matter how many times we have experienced them.

The Christmas my mother died was also my son David's first Christmas. The poignant experience of someone dying just when someone else is coming to awareness does not often occur in the same house. However, such events are going on all the time in each of our communities. As with the orchestra, these first and last times put an obligation on us to take care as we journey through this season.

Perhaps it helps to remember a child's first December, how very special we wanted that time to be. What do we want our children to experience? Excitement? Hope? The adventure of living together peacefully with compassion for each other? Gentleness? Forgiveness? Love? We may never nail it all down completely — but it doesn't hurt to try!

DECEMBER 20
A SOLSTICE FOR ALL

When I think of the winter solstice today, I imagine hilltops. Many years ago I lived near the northern shore of San Francisco Bay and worked in the city. It was an exciting time when many people were actively reexamining their assumptions about life. Something in that time of openness led me to suggest to friends that we gather to watch the dawn on the day of the winter solstice. Almost all agreed. There may have been a mutual desire to escape the "only four more shopping days until Christmas!" mentality in the city.

So it was that about twenty people arrived at my house in the dark with blankets and thermos bottles. We walked up a nearby hill and sat in silence, looking at the stars. The spiritual types probably prayed and meditated. I did. The freethinkers just thought freely. In time, the sun began to rise over the East Bay hills. Eventually we stood up and left. The suggestion was made that we do this the next year. And we did, every year until I moved away. Why? No one ever put it into words. It was simply a very authentic moment. Our time together was the same experience for all of us and a very difference experience for each of us.

In these present days of sometimes painful cultural divide, I think back to our annual gatherings on that hill. We were atheists, Buddhists, Christians, and Jews as well as those who considered themselves ex-atheists, ex-Buddhists, ex-Christians, and secular Jews. There were some whom today we would call Evangelicals and New Agers. Some sitting there were working for radical political change. Others were convinced that change had to come from inside each person. Some wore suits during the day and others wore beads. We came up the hill from many different life directions. Yet we shared a moment together in which we somehow touched with others who had stood on other hills for thousands of years before us. Although we were very different from one another, we supported each other in our individual searches for the sacred.

Times change. I don't always go out to greet the dawn on the day of the winter solstice. But I think I would be better for it if I did.

DECEMBER 21
A TIME TO LIFT UP SOULS

The poet Rainer Maria Rilke (1875–1926) wrote that Mary

> *... climbed up the hill heavy with child,*
> *nearly without hope for solace or succor:*

These December days have been filled with the difficult experiences of people who walk the earth, as did Mary the mother of Jesus and most other mothers. As Luke tells the story, Mary, a pregnant adolescent, went to meet her cousin Elizabeth, who was in her sixth month of pregnancy. In Elizabeth's embrace, Mary's soul was lifted up.

Ours is a culture of individualism and we sometimes forget that peer-support can be a very effective tool in knocking down those walls of hopelessness. You don't have any issues like that? Well someone in the world you live in does. If you have no need to be a Mary, be an Elizabeth! Most of us would benefit from being both at times.

These are days to share our lives and our difficulties with others and to let them share with us. It may be with one other person, in a family, or in a community. We all benefit from grounding ourselves in our common humanity. There is no greater offering than the gift of hope and no better time to try to give it than today.

DECEMBER 22
EACH OF US ON A
WONDROUS FLIGHT

There are always wondrous things around us. This is a day to take the time to become aware of them — to surrender to the tempo of life outside of our preoccupations.

The mystic and poet Juan de la Cruz (1542–1591) explained Christmas as a very ordinary event. The pregnant Mary *"... will come walking down the road if you make room for her in your abode."*

I live near flyways. I can discover some marvelous sight every time I look up into the sky at this time of year. There are many migrations going on among birds large and small. I am doing what countless people have done for centuries. Three hundred years ago, a musician in Gascony also observed the many migrations and the flocks of birds on the marsh and in the mountains and wondered *"whence comes this rush of wings afar?"* all seeking the place where heaven and earth touch. The Carol of the Birds includes the lyric songs of the Nightingale and Finch as well as the hoarse chants of the Magpie and Raven, the magnificent flight of the Eagle soaring above the pudgy Partridge. Every being has a place in this *"wondrous flight."*

So do each of us.

DECEMBER 23
A PROFOUND REQUEST

Tomorrow I will help put up our crèche — a nativity scene following a practice originated by Francis of Assisi in a cave near Greccio in 1223. Around the world these displays often contain unique features. I put a little statue of St. Francis in a far corner and there are rocks collected from special places in the past. And always a rose.

In the Provence region of southeastern France, there are often found crèche figures of an old man and an old woman, clinging to each other and smiling. The legend is that this couple joined a long line of those at the crib asking for special favors. They had traveled a very long distance. What was their wish? That they both die on the same day. Why were they smiling? Because their wish was granted.

Sometimes there is truth behind Christmas fables. Perhaps this is a day to search deep within our hearts for that profound wish that defines our existence.

DECEMBER 24
O HOLY NIGHT

Tonight some of us remember a birth that blessed all the births that followed. We celebrate a new beginning, a hope. We also remember in a special way the 380,000 babies who will be born on this night. And the 150,000 of us who will end our journeys on this night.

For me, Christmas Eve is one of those times where the sacred simply flows into the ordinary moments of life. Tonight I will take a little lantern and join others walking up the very familiar path to the chapel. For me, it takes a little longer than once it did.

Here I am under the beautiful stars. Orion, my favorite constellation is high in the sky. I know that deep in a *kiva* a Hopi teenager is also watching these same stars. So is a friend standing on an ocean cliff far away. *"O Holy Night, the stars are brightly shining ...."*

As I walk in stillness among those I love, I know that wonderful choirs are beginning to sing as people file into cathedrals and churches. I also know that there are many people gazing into a fire, or sitting at the bed of a child, or someone ill. I have been at all those places and I am tonight in all those places with all of you.

Blessed be this Christmas moment for us all, for all those we love, and all the beings who are and have been and will be on earth.

DECEMBER 25
FRUSTRATA ANGELUS

O nce, long ago, I had this dream while dozing before the fire on a Christmas afternoon. Before me stood a cross-eyed, very frustrated angel with one drooping wing. He/she was going on about the task of bringing a celestial message to guys laying in the fields with their sheep.

"Shepherds are a rough, crude lot by nature. But they do understand the stars. Looking at the heavens night after night even you humans might feel a tug. After all, you were formed out of stardust. Well, I managed to get the souls of the shepherds emptied of plodding things — wool prices, girlfriends, beer, and the like. Then those souls just lifted up, and it was easy for them to experience the phenomenal awe of that night!

But your generation doesn't get it! That night is an ongoing event. The Holy Night is prolonged into every night — every birth. This night coming. Your birth.

You humans are incredibly slow to grasp that God is to be found in all the ordinary moments of life. Your cat gets it. The butterflies get it, but you don't! And I for one find that very frustrating. It would help if you would watch the margins of your life. As you are racing somewhere to do something supposedly important, a person you dash by could be involved in the most significant event on earth at that moment. Think about it!

And for heaven's sake, if you feel one of us pushing you, don't be so resistant. It can be very tiring! We are not as young as we were, you know. It really would help if you took a bit more responsibility in these matters."

Then the angel disappeared in a rather petite blaze of glory.

December 26
The Second Day Of Christmas

Hey, stop packing up the ornaments. Christmas isn't over. It is just beginning! This is St. Stephen's Day, the second of the Twelve Days of Christmas. In medieval times festivities filled all these days. Armies were forbidden to fight. Harsh nature made farming impossible. People needed a midwinter break. We still do. It would be a shame to stop everything at the end of Christmas day.

In recent years an increasing number of my friends have found ways to prolong Christmastime. Some go until the New Year and others all the way to January 5, the evening before Epiphany, the Twelfth Night. My family usually makes it up to my birthday on January 4. A few people I know take off to the ski slopes. Most of us are lucky just to have a long weekend at this time. Then it is back to our normal daytime activity. It is a matter of attitude more than anything else. To me, the week after December 25 is not the time after Christmas. It is Christmastime. I look forward to unhurriedly experiencing all the things I could never cram into December 25 which is only the first day of Christmas.

For my family, the evening meal is the special focus of the day. Around the table, we take pleasure in each other and the season. There is time to explore what these days mean for each of us.

December 27
At Home In Empty Places

It is in this time of year—when we can see the full moon through the bare branches of the trees—that many of us have found the spiritual path on which we walk into the unknown. But what about what went before?

A graduate student told me he tries to spend some time each day in a nearby cathedral but never when there is a service going on! He appreciates the sacred space but has stepped away from the denomination. To a greater or lesser degree, just about everyone I know is in a similar process.

So how do we identify and protect treasures from our spiritual heritage when there is increasing distance between ourselves and the religious communities which may have nourished us in years gone by? At no time of year is that task more challenging and more rewarding than in the month of December.

How do we find community with people on other paths? How do we help and affirm each other in our spiritual quests? The answers may be difficult to formulate but the questions themselves can enrich the annual pilgrimage we make through these days.

DECEMBER 28
RACHEL'S CHILDREN

A story in Matthew's Gospel is commemorated today in many churches. Matthew has wise men from the East coming to look for the infant King of the Jews. This mightily upsets King Herod who ordered his troops to kill all male children under the age of two in the region around Bethlehem. Then Matthew quotes a poignant verse from the prophet Jeremiah (31:15),

> *A voice was heard in Ramah,*
> *sobbing and loudly lamenting:*
> *it was Rachel weeping for her children,*
> *refusing to be comforted*
> *because they were no more.*

Did this really happen? I doubt it. But I do know that many wholly innocent children have been slaughtered during my lifetime. And it is good to remember them at this time of year.

The Children's Memorial at Yad Vashem, outside Jerusalem, is in an underground cavern. On a visit I move from the bright sunlight into a dark place filled by the sound of a recording. One and a half million children perished in the Holocaust. Their names were read out as I edged along the path. A name. The age at which the child was murdered. His or her country of origin. Then another name. Many of these children were born in the year I was born. There is an interrupted life-story behind each name.

And the slaughter is still going on in war zones and the streets of our cities. Will Rachel ever stop weeping for her children? I doubt it. So let us light a candle for all the ones we can name and for the millions whose names we do not know, and resolve to better protect our children.

December 29
Just Beyond The Horizon

Walking along a very familiar route between the olive groves and the redwood forest, I am always mindful of the relationship between myself and the community of nature around me. Whether I am aware of it or not there is a bond between myself and the decaying stump in front of me. And between me and the bird standing on the stump and looking at me! There is also a link between this present moment and all the moments I have experienced in my 85 and counting years of life. The people I have walked with before are in some ways with me now. The children I have held, and who will hold their own children in this place, are also part of this moment, and this expanded circle of existence.

Just beyond the horizon, I know that the mountains to the east are covered with snow. And west of me the great and mighty Pacific Ocean can, on a clear day, be glimpsed. That ocean is like eternity, touching people in distant lands and connecting stories of what was, is and will be.

Somehow in all of this is the reality of who I am, have been and will be. And probably the same could be said of God. Which is why on a winter day even a short walk can be holy pilgrimage.

December 30
A Missing Piece

One Christmas I had trouble with many things. A child needed to the go to the hospital emergency room on several occasions. There was worry about money problems intruding on our time. School activities, both tests and performances, were much more extensive than usual. It was a pretty hectic time without many peaceful moments.

Sometime well after Christmas Day, it came through to me that there had been very little carol singing before Christmas. The right combination of people had seldom been together at one time without an agenda of some sort. Singing those familiar songs was one of my favorite holiday activities, and I felt the lack of it. These thoughts were with me one morning when I was taking my turn with the toddler who was under the weather. I was sitting in a big rocking chair holding her. We were alone. Why not sing now? So I started singing every carol I could remember. She liked it and we kept it up for a long time, not being reluctant to repeat songs often.

I find it helpful in these late December days or nights to ask, *"What have I missed?"* Sometimes it is good to be a little eccentric at this time of year. Certainly the Bible has Mary and Joseph thinking and acting outside the box.

Okay, onward – *"Good King Wenceslas looked out, on the feast of Stephen ..."*

December 31
Breaking Through

The last day of the year. What comes to mind are champagne glasses, tuxedos, evening gowns, glittering streamers, crowds, and noise. As I don't often fit into that scene, the alternative is usually to have a time at home reflecting on things past and to come.

As I have stated before, I am very grateful to my friend Paul Clasper (1923–2011) for helping me find the spiritual road I travel. Paul was a Baptist missionary in Burma. Later he was Anglican Dean of St. John Cathedral in Hong Kong. In between, Paul was many things, including president of a College at the Graduate Theological Union. Wherever he was, Paul always considered himself a missionary, which he defined in a way that made a deep impression on me. Paul said, *"My job as a missionary is to discover how God is breaking through in cultures other than my own."*

I am not a missionary – just a pilgrim. As I have traveled through life, I have encountered many people living in different spiritual huts. Some of us grew up in huts with round windows. Some with square windows. Some huts have windows with shapes I had never before imagined!

The spiritual sunlight that comes into our huts and our lives is often determined by our windows to the light outside. I grew up in a Catholic-Christian hut. But I have learned much from a poet who grew up in a Buddhist hut. So now, standing between the past year and the one to come, I mark this moment with a poem Issa wrote at the end of December in 1819:

With confidence in the Buddha For whatever comes, I bid farewell to the departing year.

ABOUT THE AUTHOR

Tolbert McCarroll, better known as "Brother Toby", has lived by Meister Eckhart's adage that what a person acquires by contemplation should be spent in compassion. He is a highly respected spiritual guide for people on many paths and journeys.

An award-winning author of 11 books, including, *A Winter Walk, Notes from the Song of Life,* and *Childsong, Monksong,* Brother Toby is a founding member of Starcross Monastic Community. A former attorney for humanitarian causes, he has for over 50 years ventured forth in response to children and others in need. The adoptive father of several children, he also established homes for children oppressed by the AIDS pandemic in California, Romania and Africa. At Starcross he writes daily. In recent years he has had a special concern for the spiritually wounded and those at spiritual crossroads in their lives. At 85, he is increasingly looking for God in the ordinary moments of life. For several years, Brother Toby's popular *Friday Reflections* have gone out on the internet to a large following of people on all paths and of all ages (*http://www.starcross.org/reflections.htm*).

Despite occasional medical challenges, Brother Toby takes great delight in his children and grandson, nature, a cup of tea, music, his greenhouse, the olive groves, and his cat Tigger.

Grateful acknowledgements and appreciation to friends and writers for their contributions, especially to an old friend, Professor Cliff Edwards, School of World Studies at Virginia Commonwealth University, Visiting Professor at Daitokuji Monastery in Japan and Oxford University in England; author of *Christian Being and Doing*, *Van Gogh and God*, *The Shoes of Van Gogh*, *Mystery of the Night Café*, *Van Gogh's Ghost Paintings*, *Issa: The Story of a Poet- Priest*, and *The Haiku Way to Enlightenment*. Also for permission to quote from previously published materials, including: Wendell Berry's poem referenced in the March 28 reflection is copyright © 1998 by Wendell Berry, from *A Timbered Choir: The Sabbath Poems 1979–1997*. Reprinted by permission of Counterpoint. The quote of Hans Küng in the Wednesday in Holy Week reflection is from *What I Believe* copyright © Hans Küng, translated by John Bowden, 2010, Continuum Publishing. Used by permission of Bloomsbury Publishing Plc. All scriptural text is from *The Jerusalem Bible* copyright © 1966, Darton, Longman, & Todd, Ltd.

Selected Prior Comments On Tolbert McCarroll's Writings

SEASONS: *hrough a Year with a Contemporary Monastic Family*

"A kindred spirit"- **Bill Moyers**, journalist and news commentator, PBS

"Once again Brother Toby has created a rich tapestry of the ordinary and the sacred."

– **Sharon Bard**, editor of *Steeped in the World of Tea*

"*Seasons* is a very touching and heart-felt reading experience ... a kind of prayer for the living." – **Jonah Raskin**, author of *American Scream: Allen Ginsberg's Howl*

A WINTER WALK

"Every life is a story and few storytellers can capture the sense of the divine as Brother Toby can. His whole life has been a preparation for helping others face their mortality and spirituality"- **Roy M. Carlisle**, Senior Editor

THINKING WITH THE HEART: *A Monk (and Parent) Explores his Spiritual Heritage*

"A book rich in honesty, insight and compassion ... that can make our hearts more tender, more discerning and more capacious." - **Parker J. Palmer**, Quaker activist, author of *Let Your Life Speak: Listening for the Voice of Vocation*

CHILDSONG/MONKSONG: *A Spiritual Journey*

"A moving spiritual journey of a man with courage and creativity which leads to new forms of spiritual life and social involvement." - **Hans Küng**, author of *Theology for the Third Millennium: A Ecumenical View*

"A uniquely moving account of a spiritual quest into the heart of darkness. Brother Toby refuses to simplify the difficulty of doing good in a fallen world. He teaches us all how to look through the broken window at the stars. A profoundly inspiring journey." - **Paul Monette**, National Book Award author of *Becoming a Man: Half a Life Story*

"It is a story full of passion – passion that saves many lives and passion that cries out against the indifference and callousness in church and society." - **Henri J. M. Nouwen**, author of *The Wounded Healer*

"...a deeply beautiful book."- **Madeleine L'Engle**, author of *The Crosswicks Journal*

MORNING GLORY BABIES: *Children with AIDS and the Celebration of Life*

1988 CHRISTOPHER AWARD

"I read this book, and I found I had new hope again."- **Randy Shilts**, author of *And the*

Band Played On

"An extraordinary story of courage and love."- **Isabel Allende**, author of *The House of the Spirits*

"Highly recommended for all who care!" - **Elizabeth Kübler-Ross**, psychiatrist, author of *Death and Dying*

A WAY OF THE CROSS

"Both tough and comforting. He challenges and assures at the same time."- **Mario Cuomo**, former Governor of New York

GUIDING GOD'S CHILDREN: *A Foundation for Spiritual Growth in the Home*

"This is an important and magnificent book! It is clear, direct, psychologically and intellectually sound and very practical."- **Morton T. Kelsey**, author of *The Other Side of Silence*

NOTES FROM THE SONG OF LIFE: *A Spiritual Companion*

"Straightforward, yet fresh and new." - **Ernesto Cardenal**, poet, Liberation Theologian

EXPLORING THE INNER WORLD

"An invitation to remake your world from the inside out."- **National Public Radio**

Made in the USA
San Bernardino, CA
20 November 2017